Reminiscence Work
with Old People

Reminiscence Work with Old People

Clare Gillies

Principal Lecturer, School of Social Sciences
Oxford Brookes University

and

Anne James

Locality Development Manager
Oxfordshire Health and Social Services

CHAPMAN & HALL

London · Glasgow · Weinheim · New York · Tokyo · Melbourne · Madras

**Published by Chapman & Hall, 2–6 Boundary Row,
London SE1 8HN, UK**

Chapman & Hall, 2–6 Boundary Row, London SE1 8HN, UK

Blackie Academic & Professional, Wester Cleddens Road,
Bishopbriggs, Glasgow G64 2NZ, UK

Chapman & Hall GmbH, Pappelallee 3, 69469 Weinheim, Germany

Chapman & Hall Inc., One Penn Plaza, 41st Floor, New York
NY 10119, USA

Chapman & Hall Japan, Thomson Publishing Japan, Hirakawacho
Nemoto Building, 6F, 1–7–11 Hirakawa-cho, Chiyoda-ku, Tokyo 102,
Japan

Chapman & Hall Australia, Thomas Nelson Australia, 102 Dodds
Street, South Melbourne, Victoria 3205, Australia

Chapman & Hall India, R. Seshadri, 32 Second Main Road, CIT East,
Madras 600 035, India

Distributed in the USA and Canada by Singular Publishing Group Inc.,
4284 41st Street, San Diego, California 92105

First edition 1994

© 1994 Clare Gillies and Anne James
  Cover photograph copyright Jonathan Higgens 1994

Typeset in 10/12 Palatino by Mews Photosetting, Beckenham, Kent
Printed in Great Britain by Page Bros, Norwich

ISBN 0 412 58070 5   1 56593 375 3 (USA)

A catalogue record for this book is available from the British Library

Library of Congress Catalog Card Number: 94-71059

∞ Printed on permanent acid-free text paper, manufactured in
accordance with ANSI/NISO Z39.48-1992 and ANSI/NISO Z39.48-1984
(Permanence of Paper).

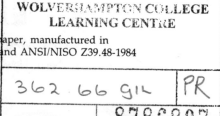

Contents

Contents

Introduction

Perhaps being old is like having lighted rooms
Inside your head, and people in them, acting
People you know, but can't quite name.

Philip Larkin

This book is about those very old people who have a great many memories but few friends left to share them with. It is about valuing and using their memories to enhance the quality of their lives, that is, about reminiscence work. Many professionals offer this help to older people, including nurses, social workers, occupational therapists and clinical psychologists, as do families and voluntary workers. Its elements can be incorporated into day-to-day contacts with older people or it may take place in more structured settings.

The transitional period from mature middle age to dependent old age is neither distinct nor precise. It does not occur at an identifiable time, it may be prolonged and it may not be obvious to the old people or their families. Loss of autonomy; the inability to cope unaided with the tasks of daily living, and increasing physical and mental frailty probably signal the area of transition. The diminished self-confidence that some old people feel at this time may be compounded by personal loss and financial difficulties; enforced changes in their lifestyles may also add to their confusion.

Reminiscence work began to be valued in the late 1960s when some professional groups became aware of the benefit to old people of under-taking a life review and in validating their life experiences. It was observed that when old people were enabled to talk about their past they became less anxious about their present situation. Sometimes both confusion and forgetfulness lessened and frail old people were able to share the present with their families and carers.

The sensitive use of memories, whether with a group or with individuals, may do much to help old people retain a good sense of self and provide a framework for a serene old age. Skill and resources are required for reminiscence work but there is no substitute for genuine interest and empathy. Listening to old people and demonstrating real interest and concerns is, in itself, comforting and therapeutic to them. However, interest and concern are not always enough when working with the wide range of individuals and characters who make up the population of old people. This book brings together academic studies and real life in order to provide the reader with a comprehensive handbook.

AUTHORS' NOTE

All the old people whose profiles appear in the book are recalled with affection. Their names and identifiable details have been changed.

ACKNOWLEDGEMENTS

Thank you to Jim and Jonathan for support and encouragement. To Tracey for typing for us. To Minky, Brian and Rosemary for their advice and comments. To Emily Leach and Robert Swanson for historical advice.

CHAPTER 1

Defining old age

WHAT IS OLD AGE?

The saying that each of us is only as old as we feel is, like most cliches, probably true. Since everyone is unique, what is brought to old age is a life constructed, though not necessarily well-constructed, from experiences, relationships and achievements that are special. In a youth-oriented society however, there are strong messages that old age and the physiological changes that it brings are not valued. These views affect the ways that old people feel about themselves and can make it difficult for them to hold on to any pride or pleasure in their lives so far.

When do people become very old? It is useful to think in terms of a life course: each stage in life is seen as part of a transitional process and not as a distinct period (Hareven and Adams, 1982). Everyone's life course is fluid and interwoven with their time in history. Each individual has to negotiate his or her own way, and the unique blend of personal experiences, relationships and family interactions are in turn influenced by changes in society. Ageing is a normal biological process which can be said to start at birth and goes on throughout the rest of life. It is not something that happens on a certain birthday and it is important to remember that the process does not speed up. Nevertheless, individuals do age at different rates and some age faster than others. The reason for this may be genetic; for example people with parents who have lived to a great age may inherit their longevity genes. More often, the speed of ageing and the levels of physical and mental fitness are determined by factors in an individual's lifestyle and in their present and previous environment. Many old people suffer chronic ill health that has been caused, not by age itself but by events earlier in their lives such as working conditions, or personal trauma. Poor diet in earlier life, due either to poverty or lack of education, can also affect health in old age (Gray and Mackenzie, 1982; Fennell, Phillipson and Evers, 1988).

Peter Laslett (1989), an academic and social historian writing when he was in his sixties, suggests that the period of retirement from paid work to death can for most people be divided into two distinct phases. To the concept of the three ages of man, childhood, adulthood and old age, he adds a fourth age: very old age. The third age is that of retirement from employment and from the responsibilities of dependent children. Laslett suggests that this should be a time of personal fulfilment. The fourth age is the time of physical degeneration ending in death, and it is from the fourth age that we get our negative images of old people as dependent, crumbling and decrepit. Laslett suggests that a positive approach to ageing aims to prolong the third age, the time of personal fulfilment, for as long as possible, and to make the fourth age as short as possible.

Laslett has been criticised sometimes as having a middle-class and Euro-centric view. However, by separating old age and retirement into two parts, the third and the fourth age, he helps to combat generalisations about old age, and to remind us that the period from retirement to death may last thirty years. 'The difficult question of the fourth age of true dependency and decrepitude, a question so closely connected with the probable length of life is [one] of the outstanding issues about ageing. It is fundamentally important to every one of us, at whatever stage of the life course we happen to be.' (Victor, 1987). An individual's experience of ageing must be set in its cultural and social context, as a socially defined experience.

Old people become vulnerable when they are no longer able to care for themselves, when they have lost much of their independence and autonomy, that is, when they have left very little ability to make decisions or to see that the decisions are carried out. People of any age living on low incomes, with a poor diet, in poor housing with no prospect of employment of satisfying leisure activities are more likely to be in worse physical and mental health than those who are more fortunate and have more satisfying lives. Their independence and autonomy will be affected by these factors. Old people are no exception. As they age they carry their ever-lengthening lifetime of experiences and the legacy of their former lifestyles with them; be they good or bad, healthy or unhealthy. An important part of this legacy is their level of self-esteem, that is, how they view and value themselves.

A sense of self-worth or self-esteem depends heavily on the value friends, neighbours, colleagues and society put on the individual.

DEMOGRAPHY AND ETHNIC DEMOGRAPHY

In Britain in the 1990s, a fifth of the population is over retirement age. Between 1981 and the year 2001 the number of people aged 85 and over is expected to rise from half a million to over one milion. There is an increasing number of families of three and four generations living in Britain now. This means that the 'shape' of the population has changed. When the birth rate is high and there are, in percentage terms, few old people, the population is shaped like a triangle, with large numbers of young people at the base of the triangle and comparatively few old people at the peak. When the birth rate drops and the percentage of old people increases, the shape becomes rectangular, with the numbers of old and young being more equal. There is a general concern about this new rectangular-shaped population, fuelled by the assumption that everyone who is retired is frail, and therefore will need a place in a residential or nursing home or depend on relatives to care for them (Fennell, Phillipson and Evers, 1988).

The 1991 census, which gave 32 categories of ethnicity, showed that there are now more than three million people from ethnic minorities in Britain, almost 5% of the population. Indians form the largest group with 840 000, followed by Caribbeans (499 000), Pakistanis (475 000) and Black Africans (207 000). Very old people are averagely represented in some ethnic groups, for example, in line with the percentage for the population as a whole, 18% of Jews are over retirement age, but are under-represented in others. Only around 2% of the Pakistani population is over retirement age. Although nationally the numbers of very old people from ethnic minorities are small, the concentration in some parts of the country of ethnic groups creates a particular need for local provision specific to those communities (OPCS, 1991).

It is important to address the situation in which very old people from ethnic minorities find themselves. Many of them are at risk on three counts: because they are old, because of the physical conditions and hostility under which they have to live, and because, often, services are not accessible to them (Norman, 1985). Old people from ethnic minorities may find that their survival to very old age away from their homeland has not led to the hallowed role that they had expected. Glendenning (1979, p. 15) quotes the Brent Indian Association:

> The Asian elderly [man] has witnessed his world gone topsy-turvy. His family got scattered all over the world. His physical environment was changed overnight. The economic platform upon which he stood was barbarously snatched from him. The secure cultural terrain upon which he built his psychological foundations began to totter and wobble unexpectedly. Unsteady as he stands with ebbing energies and strength even the support of a walking stick thrust into his hands by local charities could not help him balance.

Just as the experiences of the native British population vary widely, so do those of immigrant populations. In order to understand old

Defining old age

people from ethnic minorities we need to look back 50, 60 or 70 years
to where they have come from, to their earlier lives, and to their diverse
geographic, cultural, racial and social origins. Chapter 8 gives some
background to four ethnic groups/countries, information which, in
addition to being of use in its own right, will also give an idea of the
spread of information needed in order to understand what men and
women from ethnic minority groups have brought to their maturity.
For example, the Barbadian man who came to Britain in the 1950s in
response to London Underground's recruiting drive will differ from
the Hong Kong Chinese peasant farmer who came to Britain in the
1960s to open a restaurant. The experiences of the Kenyan Asian
woman whose family came to Britain in the 1960s after the Kenyan
government confiscated Asians' property and businesses and drove
them out will not be the same as those of the Jewish couple who arrived
in Britain in 1939, fleeing from Nazi persecution. In addition, people
from the same culture can have widely differing experiences. The
Sylheti men from Bangladesh who travelled the world working as
seamen may have ended up in London towards the end of their lives,
but they have quite different histories to the Sylheti men who came
to settle in Britain in the 1960s and 1970s and sent for, or brought with
them, wives and families.

DEPENDENCY

For many very old people their security and confidence revolve around
a relatively small number of supports and services; any withdrawal
or disruption of these can lead to confusion, depression and an
inability to cope. Old people experience the 'structured dependence'
(Stevenson, 1989) of human beings on one another and on society.
Stevenson uses this term to describe the relationships that people need
to survive and flourish. People depend on a range of organisations,
services and individuals as diverse as public utilities, local pubs,
neighbours and milkmen. If one part of the structure fails they turn
to another. This structured dependence has become increasingly
complex in the late twentieth century. Stevenson writes 'the analysis
of the factors leading to structured dependency in old age is a powerful
one, bound up with economic policies which are determined as always
by values and essentially moral choices about priorities. Some government statements have come perilously close to saying that we cannot
afford old people.'

The government's 'Care in the Community' legislation requires local
authorities to assess elderly people, including the very old and
vulnerable. Following an assessment that identifies needs, the local
authority is required to construct a 'package of care' in partnership

with the old person and their carers, in order to restore their structured dependency. Whilst this is a laudable aspiration in theory, what often happens in practice is that the local authority has insufficient money to meet the needs of everyone seeking their help, so people who still have some ability to cope will not receive services. In addition those services that are on offer may do little to enhance the dependent person's self-esteem and ability to cope and, in some cases, they may even diminish it. The majority of community care services still need to take greater account of what their clients say they want. Too often day care, for example, is provided to contain an elderly person in order to give carers or neighbours a break, but little attention is paid to the quality of the experience for the person (Stevenson, 1989). Reminiscence work could form a valuable and pleasurable part of day care for such people.

The negative stereotype of old and very old people leads many to assume that most of them are disabled, totally dependent, and live in residential or nursing homes. However, only 8% of people aged 75 or over live in residential care, the other 92% live in the community, many coping with no help or very little help from others. Although, undoubtedly, dependency and disability do increase with age, the most severe levels of disability remain low until people are over 70. A national study in 1986 showed that over the age of 85, 52% of old people were able still to go out of doors unaided, and only 31% needed help to get up and down stairs (Family Policy Study Centre, 1991).

Many people in late old age do have impaired hearing and sight. Some may never have been able to hear well or have always had only restricted sight, and they may therefore have adjusted to this when they were younger. For a significant number, however, intervention or treatment that provides the right glasses or hearing aid, or even ear syringing, can make an enormous difference. Not being able to hear or see well can mean acute loneliness. Casual conversations are limited, and radio, television and books – great comforts to most lonely people – may no longer be of any value. Younger people too are often inhibited in engaging with people who cannot hear or see because easy contact and discussions are no longer possible. Such old people are therefore thrust back into their own restricted world, and the isolation can put them at risk of developing depression or other mental health problems.

LOSS

When considering loss, death and bereavement in very old people, Stevenson (1989) draws on existential philosophy, a view that holds 'a human existence is composed of all the choices of action [eg: desires, attachments] made up from moment to moment'. This model views life as a constant juggling act of demands: pulls from relationships, clashing environmental factors, and conflicting feelings from within oneself. Part of the juggling act is coping with the fact that pain and pleasure can co-exist in the same event. The act of juggling helps to bring the contradictions of life together in a way that makes it possible to cope with them. People, of whatever age, who are in touch with their own feelings and with reality are the successful jugglers. They will tolerate, cope, and even grow when faced with pain, uncertainty, anxiety and loss, because they can integrate these experiences into their lives. They can also face death with equanimity. People often talk about a 'good' death, where dying becomes a final act of personal growth. For those people not in touch with reality however, the anxieties and changes that life brings may be very difficult, and they may cope by trying to ignore them. For very old people the collapse of their structured dependency network, a network that is vulnerable as it depends on comparatively few people and resources, may result in total personal collapse, destructive suffering and difficult behaviour. The increased death rate of widowers in the months after the death of their wives seems to underline this point (Young, Benjamin and Wallis, 1963; Murray Parkes, Benjamin and Fitzgerald, 1969). This self-destructive sadness is particularly poignant in those old people whose security, hitherto, has depended solely and rigidly on the routine and objects of daily living, rather than the integration of experiences.

Prior to retirement, work, either in the home or paid employment, will have taken up the bulk of most adults' waking hours. Work gives people an important part of their identity, for example, most people are asked on a first meeting what they do for a living. Retirement from paid employment can mean three important losses for the individual: the loss of a time-consuming and often satisfying activity (resulting in a great deal more leisure time), the loss of identity and role, and often, though not always, financial loss (Victor, 1987). Many people adjust to the losses of retirement and make full and enjoyable use of their increased leisure, but it is on the whole something that they have to do for themselves without help from others. Laslett suggests that the negative images that society has created of old age have meant pensioners have had to try and create their own positive images in the face of an unsympathetic society.

Loss is a pervasive part of extreme old age. Very old people will have faced many losses: spouse, partner, friends, neighbours, their life's work, their independence and maybe even their home. In order to cope they will need to have grieved properly and completely in order to come to terms with their losses and integrate the effects into their lives. Much has been written about the grieving process, a process first identified by Lindemann (1944), who described the bereaved person as 'depressed and apathetic with a sense of futility. Associated symptoms are insomnia, anorexia, restlessness, irritability with occasional outbursts of anger directed at others or the self.'

More recent writers on this subject (Murray Parkes, 1972; Pincus, 1976; Kübler-Ross, 1978) all of whom have worked with bereavement, stress the importance of a period of mourning to the health of anyone who has been bereaved. That is, a time to be sad and to be angry, to come to terms with the loss by facing the consequences of no longer having the loved person in their lives. They argue that until this is done – and it cannot be done quickly – no one can start to re-build their lives or make helpful new relationships.

For many, religious faith is a way of making sense of existence and experience, and of shaping moral codes and perceptions of self and others. Earlier in the century religion was more central in most people's lives, and when working with very old people it is important to take this into account. Religious beliefs and customs are extremely important in helping people to come to terms with loss and bereavement. When working with someone whose religious or cultural beliefs are unfamiliar it is extremely important to get advice from an appropriate religious leader, a priest, rabbi, imam for example. A very useful publication, the Shap Calendar of Religious Festivals, gives details of the major religions. Green and Green (1991) comprehensively cover religious, ethnic and cultural aspects of death and dying.

MENTAL HEALTH

Mental health problems or mental illness can, and usually does, result in changes in the individual's social or emotional behaviour, and their perceptions of the world. The underlying causes of these changes may be environmental (a change in circumstances), personal or emotional (a change in self), physical and organic, or all three. Changes with environmental or personal and emotional causes are usually reversible. Physical or organic changes (such as dementia) are not. Around 6% of people over 65 and 18% of people over 80 suffer from some form of dementia, but many old people suffer from mental health problems that are not organic. The percentage of over 65 year olds suffering from depression is generally thought to be around 15%, with 3–4% suffering from major depressions. However, some researchers believe that the true incidence of depression in this age group may be as high as 44%, with many depressive illnesses among old people going undetected (Family Policy Studies Centre, 1991). Other psychiatric illnesses occurring less frequently are generalised anxiety disorders, phobic disorders, paranoid illnesses, and drug and alcohol dependencies. And people who have had mental health problems in earlier life may well bring those problems with them into their very old age.

The social isolation experienced by some old people can, and often does, lead to depression and to a diminished ability to communicate and be sociable. These old people are likely to be housebound, going out rarely and probably seeing few people. The majority of their visitors will be professionals, who have called to do a job and not to chat with them or be social. Depression and diminished social and communication skills work in a vicious circle, each reinforcing the other. Reminiscence, with individuals or groups, can be an excellent way of helping lonely old people to regain their social and communication skills, and these in turn can help them to combat depression. Similarly, a life history book made with a great-grandchild, a young neighbour or secondary school pupil can help by demonstrating care and respect for that person and their past and by creating an opportunity for genuine conversation and social interaction. It is important to establish the ability and, more importantly, the willingness of a particular old person to take part in reminiscence or life history work. Each person is unique and two people with the same diagnosis (of severe dementia for example) may react completely differently, one gaining and giving a great deal while the other remains impervious. Clear, effective communication is crucial to all reminiscence and life history work. How to communicate and what behavioural signs and indicators to look out for are discussed in Chapters 3 and 4.

Mental health problems are no bar to enjoying a reminiscence group. The inability of some very old people with no short-term memory to recall recent events such as being part of a reminiscence group, can suggest that there is very little value in reminiscence. However, Lazarus' research (1976) showed that encouraging geriatric patients to talk about 'the old days' helped to lift depression and renewed pride in past achievements. Tobin (1991, cited in Bornat 1994) showed that 'making the past vivid, particularly in the presence of a sympathetic listener, can be one of the key resources very old people use in maintaining their psychological health'. Most workers who have been part of a reminiscence group for withdrawn old people have little doubt about the value of the experience for all who take part. A young, newly-qualified nurse on a psycho-geriatric in-patient unit was won over to this work by her experience of a reminiscence group. The group was led by an occupational therapist who used old household objects such as flat irons, some curling tongs and dolly-pegs as a means of bringing the past to the minds of the old people. She talked a little about each object and then passed it to the group member nearest to her. They in turn were asked to pass it to their neighbour telling them if they had ever had or used such a thing. Objects were passed round the whole group in this way with members talking and even joking about them. The combination of touching, talking and sharing resulted in a happy and lively atmosphere. The group ended with animated faces, smiles and goodbyes and wishes to see each other again soon. The young nurse left the room and returned a short time later. All was silent, the members of the group who remained in the room had returned to their isolated, inward-looking worlds, and no one appeared have any recollection of her or of the good time that she had shared with them. However, later when she was bathing Mrs Smith who had been in the group she asked her about wash days. Mrs Smith smiled, something she did rarely, and talked a little about the wash days she remembered.

It is wise to seek advice, however, before setting up a group or undertaking a life history book with people who appear to have mental health problems. If it is needed, help will be readily available in a psychiatric setting from a community psychiatric nurse (CPN), or other psychiatric professionals. If there is uncertainty about the old person's mental abilities, the Hodgkinson Mental Test Score (MTS) can be useful. This ten-question test was devised for elderly people and it is widely used. It is not very sensitive to minor changes in ability or understanding, but it gives a good indication of mental functional ability, and is easy to administer. The significant score is seven; if an old person scores less than seven there is probably something wrong. All the scores must be considered in the light of what regular carers say and what has been learned about the old people and their attitudes from observation and records (Hodgkinson, 1972).

Mental Test Score (MTS)
Score one for each correct answer. Total the points for the final score.

1. How old are you?
2. What is the time to the nearest hour (without looking at a clock or watch)?
3. Give the person an address eg: 42 West St. Ask them to repeat the address at the end of the test.
4. What year is it?
5. Give your home address, or the name of the hospital or home where you live.
6. Recognise two people known to you.
7. What is your date of birth?
8. In what year did World War I start?
9. Name the present monarch.
10. Count backwards from 20 to 1.

The results of this test can show how much in touch with reality the old person is and if specialised help is needed. It will not necessarily help to build up a profile of the old person's needs in the way that discussion about their past or their social functioning or social contacts will. Readers particularly interested in mental health and reminiscence will find that Marshall's book *Working with Dementia* (1990) gives helpful checklists and guidance towards assessment of the older person, and Bornat's book *Reminiscence Reviewed* (1994) is useful for work with old people with dementia, depression, or other mental health problems.

SUMMARY

Defining old age is not easy: everyone is different and old age does not happen suddenly. Ageing is a process that lasts throughout adult life, and what is brought to old age is a unique combination of experiences. For most people the greater part of old age is spent in active retirement, and for many it is a time of fulfilment, even though negative attitudes in society may undermine this. For a significant minority, however, the quality of their lives is curtailed either because they lack the personal, social or financial resources to gain fulfilment or because they have chronic physical or mental health problems. It is to the plight of this minority that this book addresses itself, people who are old and vulnerable, some of them prematurely. It looks at ways of using reminiscence, with both individuals and groups, to help old people make the most of their diminishing physical and mental abilities, and in doing so, to enable them to contribute the unique gift of themselves and their experiences to the world around them.

REFERENCES

Bornat, J. ed. 1994. *Reminiscence Reviewed: Perspectives, Evaluations, Achievements.* Open University Press, Milton Keynes.

Family Policy Study Centre. 1991. *An Ageing Population.* Factsheet 2. Family Policy Study Centre. Baker St, London.

Fennell, G., Phillipson C., and Evers, H. 1988. *The Sociology of Old Age.* Open University, Milton Keynes.

Glendenning, F., ed. (1979). *The Elders in Ethnic Minorities.* Beth Johnson Foundation, Stoke on Trent.

Gray, M. and Mackenzie, H. 1982. *Caring for Older People.* Penguin, Harmondsworth.

Green, J.B. and Green, M.A. 1991. *Dealing with Death.* Chapman and Hall, London.

Hareven, T.K. and Adams, T. 1982. *Ageing and Life Course Transitions: an Interdisciplinary Perspective.* Tavistock, London.

Hodgkinson, H.M. 1972. Evaluation of a Mental Test Score for assessment of mental impairment in the elderly. In *Age and Ageing*, **1**, 233–8.

Kübler-Ross, E. 1978. *On Death and Dying.* Tavistock, London.

Laslett, P. 1989. *A Fresh Map of Life: the Emergence of the Third Age.* Weidenfeld and Nicolson, London.

Lazarus, L.W. 1976. Program for the elderly at a private psychiatric hospital. In *Gerontologist*, **16**, 125–131.

Lindemann, E. 1944. Symptomatology and the management of acute grief. In *American Journal of Psychiatry*, **101**, 141.

Marshall, M., ed. 1990. *Working with Dementia.* Venture Press, Birmingham.

Murray Parkes, C., Benjamin, B. and Fitzgerald, R.G. 1969. Broken Heart: a study of increased mortality among widowers. In *British Medical Journal*, **1**, 740–743.

Murray Parkes, C. 1972. *Bereavement, Studies of Grief in Adult Life*. Tavistock, London.

Norman, A. 1985. *Triple Jeopardy: Growing Old in a Second Homeland*. Centre for Policy on Ageing, London.

Office of Population Censuses and Surveys (OPCS). 1991. *1991 Census*. HMSO, London.

Pincus, L. 1976. *Death and the Family, the Importance of Mourning*. Faber and Faber.

Rose, N. 1989. *Essential Psychiatry*. Blackwell Scientific Publications, Oxford.

Shap Calendar of Religious Festivals. Shap Working Party on World Religions, West Sussex Institute of Higher Education, Bishop Otter College, Chichester, West Sussex.

Stevenson, O. 1989. *Ageing and Vulnerability – A Guide to Better Care*. Age Concern, London.

Victor, C.R. 1987. *Old Age in Modern Society*. Chapman and Hall, London.

Wilkin, D. and Thompson, C. 1989. *Users' Guide to Dependency Measures for Elderly People*. University of Sheffield, Unit for Social Services Research.

Young, M., Benjamin, B. and Wallis, C. 1963. Mortality of Widowers. In *The Lancet*, **2**, 454.

CHAPTER 2

Reminiscence work and oral history

Reminiscence work and oral history are different and both are valid and valuable. It is possible to engage in reminiscence as a validating experience for an individual whilst enriching historical knowledge with details from old people's stories. It is important however to understand the difference between the two. Reminiscence work concerns itself primarily with the social and personal benefits for the individuals concerned and not with the documenting of history. Oral history is primarily concerned with the individual's oral contribution to documenting history. However, reminiscence, even with people with limited communication skills and little or no short-term memory, can produce a treasure-house of information and insights. Some of these may be of sufficient general interest to make a contribution to the recording of the past, although this is not usually the case.

REMINISCENCE WORK

Reminiscing is a commonplace and normal activity. It is something that we all do frequently. Everyone has stories to tell about their past experiences and about their perception of or reaction to world events. Recounting such stories can be immensely pleasurable both to the raconteur and to the listener; it can also be cathartic or therapeutic. It can occur spontaneously and indeed often does; for example, when former colleagues meet each other unexpectedly and talk about where they used to work and the people they used to work with, or when a granddaughter finds old family photographs as she helps her grandmother to spring clean and asks about the family that they share, or when members of the local British Legion club recall their time as soldiers together in the North African desert. Reminiscence can occur as a result of an organised event, for example, at a school or class reunion, or when a grandfather takes his grandchildren to visit the village where he grew up and the house in which he was born.

Some people, however, need skilled help, support and encouragement in order to help them reminisce. The essence of this kind of help is social, it facilitates communication and companionship amongst people who may be isolated because they are in a new and unfamiliar situation. In addition, they may be confused because they have little short-term memory, or lack social skills because they are out of practice in dealing with social interactions. Normally very uncommunicative people are able to talk in a lively and realistic manner about their past when stimulated by planned reminiscence. Coleman (1989) warns against evaluating the benefits of reminiscence only as a pleasing activity and thus avoiding looking at the potential it has for an individual's overall psychological adjustment.

Although now widely practised, reminiscence work has only comparatively recently become established as a valid way of working with old people. Of the research studies undertaken some demonstrate its value; others, however, are inconclusive (Coleman, 1989). Nevertheless, the anecdotal evidence from the large number of workers and old people who have used reminiscence emphasise its worth. Psychotherapy has always acknowledged the importance of validating life experiences in old age particularly in relation to approaching death (Jung, 1934; Freud, 1914). Erikson, writing in 1950, developed a theory of the stages of life, giving importance to integrity in old age. He described the last stage of human development as one in which a person achieves integrity or experiences despair. Integrity is reached by looking back over one's life and determining that it had been worthwhile, that one had occupied a unique place in time, and was satisfied with life as one had lived it. Coleman (1989, p. 156) endorses the role that religion has in achieving integrity, suggesting that 'It is foolish of psychologists to ignore religious discussion of forgiveness and also the healing of tragic and hurtful memories.'

Despite both psychology and religion emphasising the importance of time spent in old age reviewing one's life and making comfortable sense of it, reminiscence was not encouraged in the 1950s and 1960s. It was felt that if people lived in the past they would lose touch with the present (Kaminsky, 1984). Disengagement theory put forward by Cumming and Henry (1961) suggested that ageing was a many sided process with no defined beginning or ending, but with society gradually making fewer demands on the old person and they, for their part, gradually withdrawing from life. As reminiscing was seen as evidence of withdrawal from everyday life and even preparation for death it was discouraged (Dobrof in Kaminsky, 1984).

The change of heart about reminiscence is nicely illustrated by Havinghurst, an eminent psychologist in the field of ageing, who in

1959 advised old people to avoid reminiscences and by 1972 was researching its benefits. Butler (1963) is regarded as the pioneer of this change. He describes the review of one's past life as a normal and necessary task of old age and as an opportunity to revisit unresolved conflicts and resolve them. He saw life review as an important stock-taking exercise. By the late 1960s and 1970s, psychologists, social workers and psychiatrists were starting to use life review and the validation of life experiences in old age in their work with old people. Although large numbers of old people undertaking life review and reminiscence were not able to cope well with everyday memories, their memories of events long ago were not impaired. It was found that by exercising memory and talking about those long-past experiences old people became less anxious about their current disorientation and, sometimes, their disorientation and forgetfulness lessened (Butler, 1963; Kaminsky, 1984). They appeared more alert and responsive, looked happier and talked more freely to their peers. Holland and Rabbitt (1991) suggest that the more a person is prompted to remember, the better his or her ability to do so. In Britain, reminiscence was 'launched' by the Reminiscence Aid Project in 1978–9, funded by the government and focusing on residents and patients in homes and hospitals in the London area. Its objectives were to provide 'a framework for caring interactions' and for old people 'to regain a fuller perspective of their own past lives, the better to relate to the present'. The project's intention was to produce a slide/tape collection that would increase reminiscence in elderly, mentally infirm people. When government funding ended and the project moved to the Help the Aged Education Department in 1981, they in turn produced six slide/tape sequences (their Recall Packs). Demand for the sequences was overwhelming: reminiscence was established (Bornat, 1994).

The bulk of reminiscence work takes place in residential institutions or hospitals. Coleman (1986) pioneered reminiscence work in the community in the 1970s, with his studies of old people living alone in sheltered housing, studies that spanned years. Reminiscence is now, of course, accepted as a normal and valid activity in a wide variety of community settings. Coleman's was the first major study of old people who were able to live independent lives, had not been assessed as in need of 24-hour care or admitted to a hospital or institution. His findings give helpful guidance about what old people are likely to bring to and expect from reminiscence. He found that between a quarter and a third of his respondents reported that they lived in the past, two-thirds to three-quarters reported that they liked to think about the past. The latter group had a much higher morale and more positive outlook than the former. He found too, that whilst the majority of elderly people were happy to think and talk about the past, a significant minority were either troubled by doing so, saw no point in it, or could not bear it. Clearly reminiscence work would not be appropriate for these people, or indeed welcomed by them. However, as stated elsewhere in this book and in other texts, it is important to establish with the individuals with whom you are hoping to work that they are willing and able to take part in life history and reminiscence work. Bender (in Bornat, 1994) reckoned that one third of patients with severe dementia living in continuing care units would benefit from reminiscence work. However, he cautions that everyone is different, and the proportion of patients who could benefit may be much higher than this in some units.

In summary, the scientific evidence of the value of reminiscence work is at best equivocal. Practitioners of reminiscence work need to accept this and not let it deter them from exploring its value to the old people with whom they are working. The focus of reminiscence remains personal and social; its importance as an activity will vary from individual to individual, and that value cannot always be seen in the immediate setting.

ORAL HISTORY

At the same time as the social work and psychiatric professions were exploring the social and therapeutic use of memory, oral history was being established as an important community activity. Compiling oral history was seen as an activity that ordinary people could do which had the potential to contribute to academic study (Thompson, 1992; Humphries, 1984). The oral tradition, that is, the tradition of passing on information by word of mouth from generation to generation, is the oldest way of recording the past. This long tradition of sharing memories means that the spoken word is at the heart of the way in which history was recorded and passed on from generation to generation. Our history, our heritage and our traditions all owe their origins to the oral tradition and to older generations telling younger ones about the past.

Afro-Caribbeans have kept alive African stories, beliefs and legends through the oral tradition. Australian aborigines pass knowledge about their geography of the landscape and their history through 'song lines'. Religious beliefs and traditions worldwide also depend heavily on the oral tradition. The Venerable Bede, the eighth-century English Christian monk and scholar, wrote in his *Ecclesiastical History of the English People*, 'I am not dependent on any one author but on countless faithful witnesses who either know or remember the facts.' Christian scholars tell us that the writing of the gospels of Matthew, Mark, Luke and John was not started until at least 30 years after the death of Jesus Christ and when the gospels were written they inevitably relied heavily on the oral tradition and reminiscences of members of the early church. This accounts in part for the different stories that are told in the different gospels, that is, people told the gospel writers what they could remember.

Throughout history people's memories have been used to document events; historians used the oral tradition – folklore, songs, rhymes and stories – in order to create rich and full written pictures that weave together material from a range of sources showing us what that material or information has in common and what is unique about it. However, by the end of the 19th century, in the West the oral tradition had been downgraded as an acceptable historical resource, and was lost to society. History had become a 'serious' study with accepted academic methods and principles, to which the written word was central. Oral testimonies were no longer regarded as legitimate; only amateurs used spoken testimonies and stories. This in turn affected the way history was taught to children, who were educated to believe that the lives and memories of ordinary people had no place in official histories (Thompson, 1992). This will probably strike a chord with older readers when they think back to how they were taught history at school. They will probably think of dates, kings and queens, and Acts of Parliament, that is, a dry catalogue which had little to do with creating an interest in or an understanding of the people who lived that history and of the things that shaped their lives. This happened both in Britain and in the British colonies where children were taught British history; consideration was rarely given to local cultures or local history and traditions. Indeed, in many colonies 'history' only started once the Union Jack was flying. The net effect of this was the distancing of history from memory and the devaluing of the oral tradition as a gift that could be passed from one generation to another.

History, as recorded by historians and reinforced by taught history, is largely political and administrative in its focus. However, 'reality is complex and many-sided; and it is a prime merit of oral history that . . . it allows the original and multiplicity of standpoints to be recreated' (Thompson, 1992, p. 5). In the 1950s attitudes started to change. Oral history started to regain its credibility as a respectable practice. George Ewart-Evans (1956 in Thompson, 1992) the first modern British oral historian, worked in East Anglia in the 1950s recording rural life: he talked to farm hands and farm workers about life and tradition in their areas. The title of his first book was *Ask The Fellows Who Cut The Hay*, which is exactly what he did in order to collect material for the book. By the 1960s the universities of Essex and Kent were using interviews with large numbers of older people in historical surveys. This work was important in reinforcing oral history as academically respectable and escaping from the strait-jacket that written history had imposed some hundred years earlier. Thompson can take particular credit for re-establishing the oral tradition. He writes of his belief that 'oral history gives history back to the people in their own words. And in giving a past it helps them towards a future of their own making' (Thompson, 1992, sleeve comment).

The growing respectability of the oral tradition was given a further boost by the development of community publishing in the early 1970s. Community publishing provided the first opportunity for ordinary people to write and have published anything from pamphlets to books that were biographical and often contained reminiscences about their early lives and the communities in which they still lived. Publishing projects were often resourced by teachers, who, working with community activists, helped people who were unused to using the written word to create highly readable accounts from their oral reminiscences. In addition to resourcing academic study, the pamphlets and books proved fascinating to people currently living in those communities, not only newcomers to the area, but also people who had grown up and lived all their lives there.

Oral history also provides a way of documenting and validating the experiences of older people from other countries, as beautifully demonstrated in Age Exchange's book *A Place to Stay: Memories of Pensioners from Many Lands* (Schweitzer, 1984). The history or local studies sections of public libraries will almost certainly have local publications. Photographs have a part to play too. An enchanting example is 'World Famous Round Here', a photographic record of life in the South Yorkshire mining village of Fryston between the wars using some of the thousands of photographs taken by local man Jack Hulme, accompanied by his descriptions of life and events. He included descriptions by ex-residents of Fryston:

> Jack was trusted by the people he photographed. He was familiar enough for his camera to be almost unnoticed. So his pictures are for the most part intimate, unposed and unselfconscious. Few collections of photographs have such a value as a social history, though it would be wrong to imagine that they have no further aesthetic worth. Some explore gentle surrealism – Jack's own mother asleep on her couch with floral wall paper blooming dreamily around her, a woman in her best summer frock sitting in a field with a gas mask on her head, a lone fiddler stumbling on his crutches with his violin hung around his neck (Van Riel *et al.*, 1990, introduction, pp. iv–v).

REMINISCENCE WORK AND ORAL HISTORY

Readers may refer to the Oral History Society's bi-annual journal which brings together current work with research articles on reminiscence and oral history. A note of caution, however: the memories that old people will share as part of reminiscence and life history work will be fascinating; what they may not be is significant enough in a local or national context to be worth a historian collecting. In addition, people's lack of memory or communication problems may make what they are saying difficult to record and to validate, which makes them unreliable sources from a historian's point of view. This sounds less harsh, when illustrated in the following two profiles.

May in her late 80s was extremely confused. She lived in a residential home. The home started a reminiscence group which she appeared to enjoy but to which she contributed little other than smiles and pleasantries. One week the group set up the lounge as a cinema and showed a Charlie Chaplin film. May came alive: 'I know him, he lived in our part of London, . . . we were all very poor . . . he went to America, he was famous, but he came back to see us you know.' All that May said about Charlie Chaplin was true – this can be established from other sources – but she was unable to give any more detail when questioned by excited staff. She could not even give her own address at that time, or any consistent details about her family. Her confusion made her an unreliable source of information for documenting history.

George, on the other hand was also in his late 80s. He was physically very frail, a bit forgetful from day to day, and a stroke had left him emotionally labile and he cried very easily. However his long-term memory was excellent. He was able to contribute detail about everyday life to reminiscence discussions, and to set that detail in a historical context of events both local and national. During a reminiscence group session in the residential home in which he lived, he told how he clearly remembered seeing the eminent Victorian photographer Henry Taunt at work in Oxford; remembered how Taunt paid boys to carry all the equipment a photographer needed in those days, and how he set about taking pictures. The Oxfordshire County Museum Service has a Henry Taunt Collection of photographs and photographic plates and the curator was extremely keen to record George's memories. George had something unique to contribute to the museum's archives, and the curator knew George would be a reliable source of accurate new information.

The experience of reminiscence was valuable to both May and George but only George was able to make a contribution to oral history. For May, the weekly reminiscence sessions gave her a time to be sociable, something which her confusion made hard at other times and it created a bond between her and the care staff who loved to ask her about the stories that she sometimes told in the group. For George, it validated him as an important person with a contribution to make, something which recently his frailty and strokes had denied him. For the museum service there was the bonus of George's contribution to their archival material.

Oral history and the oral tradition have been re-established as legitimate approaches to recording the past and many museums now have their own oral history archive to which community initiatives contribute. There are major oral history collections in large museums in Bradford and Southampton and a national record at the National

Sound Archive in London. If an old person seems to have something special to contribute as George did, it is worth contacting the local museum service or a history teacher for their advice. It is important to make sure that the person concerned actually wants to make a contribution.

An excellent example of reminiscence that was both a valuable experience for individual people and a contribution to recorded history is described in an article entitled 'It's not true what was written down; Experiences of Life in a Mental Handicap Institution', (Fido and Potts, 1989). The authors contrast information recorded in the institution's official documents with the memories of people's experiences as inmates of that institution. The 17 people they interviewed were able to see for themselves, perhaps for the first time, that they were individuals who mattered and that what they said could be believed and was of interest. At the same time, they added to our understanding of what the enforcement of the Mental Deficiency Act 1913 meant in practice. This Act enshrined the fears and prejudices of the time that led mental defectives, who today would be called people with learning disabilities, to be regarded as the cause of most social evils and a major economic burden. People certified as defective under the Act were graded, as 'idiot', 'imbecile', or 'feeble-minded'. There was another category, that of 'moral defective'. It was generally believed that high-grade mental defectives, the feeble-minded, were the real social menace and most likely also to be moral defectives. Many people, often in their teens, who would now be considered as having a mild learning disability, or who had committed a minor offence, or were single mothers, would be labelled feeble-minded and a moral defective and sent to live permanently in an institution. It is not unusual nowadays to find residents in homes for elderly people who arrived at those homes on their discharge aged 60 or 65 from mental hospitals and long-stay mental handicap hospitals where they had been all their lives because they were, for example, supposed to have stolen money from an employer, or had been in service and become pregnant by their employers.

All the people Fido and Potts interviewed remembered clearly the traumatic process of being certified and admitted to the institution. Despite the fact that the handbook in the institution's archives advised officers that they must establish a friendly and sympathetic bond with patients, the executive officer of that institution was someone of whom all the interviewees had been afraid and with whom they were all angry. They also threw light on the punishment regimes, and on the cruel segregation of men and women born of the fear that, particularly if the moral defectives mixed, they might have a child thus creating another burden and expense for the state. The poignancy of these people's stories told in their own words creates for the first time in the recorded history of that institution a picture of what it felt like to be an individual locked up and deprived of rights and dignity. This picture cuts through the official written and photographic evidence of the institution, for example, the group photograph Fido and Potts use in their article that presents calm, ordered row upon row of inmates with bland, submissive faces.

Another example of reminiscence and oral history combining is seen in work done by Black and Afro-Caribbean groups of old people on their experience of arriving in post-war Britain. During the 1950s, industry, London Underground and the NHS all recruited people from the West Indies to come to work in Britain. The immigrants' stories reveal racial prejudice and appalling living conditions, providing a contrast to the official history, which, in the colonial spirit of the time, shows Britain as the Mother Country providing opportunities for West Indians.

> When I came [to Britain], he [my husband] was very sad because he did not have a proper house to put me into. The landlady said we could not walk through the front door, we had to go through the back, and no-one could visit there. He bought a right big basin and said it's in here you have to wash, 'cos they are not going to let you use the bathroom (W in Schweitzer 1984, p. 28).

SUMMARY

Both reminiscence work and oral history celebrate and use the memories of old people. The former is for the benefit of the old people themselves and, although in the telling of their stories many of them will find pride and pleasure, oral history is primarily for the benefit of others in this and following generations. This book, however, is about reminiscence work with old people, most of whom will not have had experiences that can contribute to documented history but many of whom will enjoy the interest and respect that listening to their recollections can give.

REFERENCES

Bornat, J., ed. 1994. *Reminiscence Reviewed: Perspectives, Evaluations, Achievements*. Open University Press, Milton Keynes.
Butler, R.N. 1963. The Life Review: an interpretation of reminiscences in the aged. In *Psychiatry*, **26**, 65–76.
Coleman, P. 1986. The Past in the Present: A Study of Elderly People's Attitudes to Reminiscence. In *Oral History Journal*, **14**(1), 50–59.
Coleman, P. 1989. *Ageing and Reminiscence Processes: Social and Clinical Implications*. John Wiley and Sons, Chichester.
Cumming, E. and Henry, W.E. 1961. *Growing Old: The Process of Disengagement*. Basic Books, New York.

Erikson, E. 1950. *Childhood and Society*. W.W. Norton & Co, Inc., Boston

Fido, R. and Potts, M. 1989. It's not true what was written down: Experiences of life in a mental handicap Institution. In *Oral History Journal*, **17**, 2.

Freud, S. 1914. *The Psychopathology of Everyday Life*. Benn.

Havinghurst, R.G. and Glasses, R. 1972. An exploratory study of reminiscence. In *Journal of Gerontology*, **27**, 243–253.

Holland, C.A. and Rabbitt, P.M. 1991. Ageing Memory: Use versus Impairment. In *British Journal of Psychiatry*, **82**, 29–38.

Humphries, B. 1984 *The Handbook of Oral History: Recording Life Stories*. Interaction Imprint, London.

Jung, C.G. 1934. *The Integration of the Personality*. Routledge and Kegan Paul, London.

Kaminsky, M., ed. 1984. *The Uses of Reminiscence: New Ways of Working with Older Adults*. Haworth Press, New York.

van Riel, R., Fowler, O. and Malkin, H. eds. 1990. *World Famous Round Here: The Photographs of Jack Hulme*. Yorkshire Arts Circus, Castleford, Yorks.

Schweitzer, P., ed. 1984. *A Place to Stay: Memories of Pensioners from Many Lands*. Age Exchange, London.

Thompson, P. 1992. *The Voice of the Past: Oral History*, 2nd ed. Opus series of Oxford University Press, Oxford.

CHAPTER 3

Communicating with old people

There are many ways of improving the quality of life of old people. Some involve providing practical help to keep old people safe and comfortable and, wherever possible, to engage them in planning their own care, to enable them to feel in charge of their own lives and retain their dignity. There are other ways, one being to help older people use their long lives and their memories to engage the interest of others, to reinforce their self-esteem, and reflect upon their experiences and achievements. However one tries to help communication with very old people one must take into account their past and tap into their memories. They may not always be able to talk about the past, but understanding their present preoccupations will be easier if it is accepted that these will almost certainly be affected by, or arise from, their past experiences. In this chapter some of the barriers and aids to communication between the generations are discussed.

Whatever is discussed with the old person, it is essential that genuine interest and enquiry exist. Old people have so much to tell and their pleasure in doing so is intense. Although the fact that a man, now 85, may have left school at 13 and earned the present-day equivalent of about 40p a week is intriguing now, what is far more important is how that young man felt about leaving school at 13, and what he hoped for then, what he spent his wages on, what he had and had to do without, the quality of those early working years, and of his spare time. Genuine interest will sustain the enquirer and will be conveyed to the raconteur who will be encouraged to reflect and share precious memories.

It is not unusual to find that those whose job it is to take care of old people want to protect them and are fearful about engaging them in reminiscence work. They are afraid that reminiscence will bring up sad memories, and that even in helping old people to recall happy ones they may become painfully aware of all that they have lost.

Research into reminiscence work suggests that this is not so; depression can be lifted and recollection can aid acceptance of the present (Lazarus, 1976; Havinghurst and Glasser, 1972). In reminiscence group work, restless old people are often more attentive and less disruptive. Even very confused old people seem to be able to remember the past when prompted to do so (Kiernat, 1979). They are able to talk vividly and with humour about the past. The mood of the group members lifts, they talk and joke with each other, they become, albeit only temporarily, the people they used to be. The same reactions are apparent in work with an old person on his or her own. Friends and partners are described, sometimes lovingly, sometimes with bitterness; life events are recounted with such detail that their importance to the old person cannot be denied. Although the ability to recall and talk in ways that younger people see as rational is sometimes lost when the reminiscence session ends, it has been found that the old people are calmer and appear more content for a short time afterwards. Though they may slip back into their confusion (Lazarus, 1976), for the time spent reminiscing, they will have been able once more to communicate with other people and so have been closer to them.

Many old people quite clearly obtain great pleasure from reminiscence groups; once one has seen their enjoyment, it is easy to be convinced of the value of reminiscence. Coleman's research showed however that not all old people want to reminisce. For some the past is too painful to be recalled, for others it may no longer seem significant to their present-day lives and concerns (Coleman, 1974). Recalling painful memories may be therapeutic and sustain the self-esteem of some old people if they can be helped to remember the ways that they coped in trying situations in the past. However, for those who have deep and unresolved scars, very sensitive handling and personal counselling may be needed. Even in old age unresolved grief can be worked through but psychiatric advice should be sought if there is any doubt about this. The old people themselves will, almost certainly, make it plain if they do not want to be involved even if they no longer find it easy to express themselves clearly. It may become apparent that they do not talk about the past when it seems natural to do so, or they may convey their reluctance by their behaviour or attitude.

In extreme old age, many people have lost their close friends and partners and it is often professional carers who take on the task of helping them to assess and validate their lives. Both professional carers and younger family members can be embarrassed and worried by old people expressing strong feelings, particularly sadness; since the texture of human relationships is a tangle of losses and gains, some tears may well be shed. For people of almost any age weeping can have a restorative effect and most would consider that being close to another person is worth the risk of losing them. However, healthy sadness and regret can be confused with depression in older people; it is easy for younger people to think that anyone old must be sad because a common view is that old age is a time that is wasteful, lonely and unproductive.

Carers, both professional and family, usually consider involving old people in reminiscence when it has become clear that they are withdrawn and no longer able to help themselves. Frequently, this follows a crisis or a change in their lifestyle; possibly after they have been moved from their own home into residential care, or when they could not continue to live independently and so had to rely on others, sometimes strangers, for help with everyday life tasks. The extent of the physical and emotional changes imposed by moving is such that many old people are forced into greater dependency and even confusion. They may have just left the home where the fabric of their lives so far, and where people and events of inestimable importance to them, are represented by the personal possessions acquired over very many years. They may have left all these things behind to live communally, with strangers, in a setting that often feels bleak and bewildering no matter how much care and thought has been put into trying to make it welcoming. Daily routine may be altered drastically: they no longer cook for themselves, they can no longer potter around their own gardens, nothing is any longer where they expect it to be. A great many old people in these situations cannot adapt and become docile and sad. Residential homes where there are large rooms lined with silent old people are all too common. In situations like this it is easy to be convinced that it is kinder to leave the old people in their apathy, where they may seem unaware of their surroundings, than to prompt them to relive or recall the quality of their past lives to which they cannot return. Perhaps the greatest sadness for very old people is that there is no one left with whom they have shared their lives so far. For them to have a conversation with someone with whom they have shared only a very small part of their long lives involves effort and explanations that they may feel too weary to make. They have to be invited and encouraged to share their memories – reminiscence work can do this.

There is no doubt, as the facts given in Chapter 1 show, that some old people are deeply depressed and may need psychiatric help for this condition. For many old people, genuine interest, affection, companionship, release from practical worries such as fear of being alone, increasing interest and stimulating daily routine can be enough to lift the mood. If these things do not help, however, psychiatric advice must be sought. Signs to look for in deciding how much help is needed are a continuing sad or low mood that nothing seems to shift, frequent weeping, often without discernable cause, loss of appetite, a general feeling of being unwell, disturbed sleep patterns, for example sleeping a good deal during the day and into the evening and night but waking up very early in the morning. Sometimes confusion may indicate depression although it may have a physical cause such as an infection or even chronic constipation. Many frail old people find it difficult to express their feelings precisely, sometimes because of fatigue or difficulty in finding the right word, sometimes because they have not been accustomed to talking about themselves in this way. They more readily talk of feeling unwell, of having pain or of not being quite themselves. Although their physical condition must always be assessed, depression must also be considered. If an old person speaks of wanting to take their own life, they must not be disregarded, and specialist help must be sought. Nevertheless if an old person weeps a little when remembering something very important to them, for example the first time they held their first baby, they may well be showing that they are in touch with reality, still able to respond genuinely and openly.

The work of a Social Services care manager with Mrs Munday illustrates well the value of helping old people to express their feelings and reflect on memories tinged with sadness. Mrs Munday was an intelligent and sturdy old woman who was about to move into sheltered accommodation. She had had a sad life – three of her sons had been killed in the Second World War. As she and her care manager worked together to sort out her affairs, they found batches of photographs. As they came across pictures of each son who had died, Mrs Munday told her about him. In this way, they were able to share the pride that the ageing mother had in their achievements and her love for their foibles. One son had been tall and handsome, a fine rugby player but a flirt! The second, always jealous of his bold big brother, was a little delicate but much loved by his mother. Over the third son she felt great distress; he had been badly maimed during the war, had been unable to accept life afterwards, and had killed himself. She wept as she talked about him and seemed to relive her desperate wish to help him but 'I couldn't give him his legs back'. Her care manager asked her gently what she had been able to give him over this time and she told of their long talks, the confidences and the jokes they had sometimes shared, his weeping and her holding him. She recaptured, in other words, the times when her much-loved son and herself were closer than ever before, times of great importance to them both. She was able to acknowledge the value that her love and support had been to him. Afterwards Mrs Munday told the care manager how much she had enjoyed remembering everything, adding that she could not talk freely to her family: 'they don't like to see me upset, you see, but I can't just sort out the happy things can I?'

Mrs Munday's story underlines the point that when working with old people who are reflecting upon their lives, they will, almost inevitably, get in touch with sadness. Acknowledging this and their intense feelings dignifies them and all that they have achieved. It is hard for younger people to see someone who is old and frail become distressed. It arouses deep protective feelings and instinctively they wish to cheer them up, but this may deny them an opportunity to reflect upon, and resolve, an earlier problem.

Denying old people the right to be angry may be as limiting as denying them the right to be sad. As many people reach an advanced age, they become physically and sometimes mentally less able. Not enough is known yet about the effects of extreme age on emotional responses. Nevertheless, work with old people suggests that their emotional capacity is not diminished but their expectations of others and their own dependency may curtail the honest and healthy expression of their feelings. Reminiscence can stimulate the entire person and facilitate the expression of appropriate feelings. For the greater number of old people, reminiscence is a happy activity, and, for the younger helpers, talk of old times is enthralling.

Reminiscence work has to be approached sensitively – clear effective communication with old people requires awareness and respect for their values, as does communication between any groups of people. The skilful communicator demonstrates by a range of signals that they are listening patiently and with great attention. They should face the old person, maintain eye contact, indicate by nods and encouraging words that they are attending to them, and by facial expressions that they are in touch with the emotional impact of what is being shared (Egan, 1990). The worker must pick up hints and half-expressed ideas from body language, responding to the emotion that is shown, especially if it complements or contradicts the spoken word. For example, if someone says that they are all right but sounds hesitant and looks worried, then the non-verbal messages are almost certainly more significant than the words spoken and ought to be responded to. There is more discussion of communication skills in Chapters 4 and 5.

In addition, some knowledge of the world and culture in which the old people grew up and the concerns of their generation is essential. Communication across generations can be uneasy if the younger person does not know what life was like all those years ago but there can be additional difficulties, for example, if the young helper is white and the old person black. In communicating across cultures it is important to try to help the other person to tell about their customs and beliefs. Their experiences must be heard and respected, so if an elderly man from Jamaica talks of the racism that he has known the listener must not, out of embarrassment or shame, deny or defend this.

Although many people from ethnic minorities in this country today have lived here for three or four generations, some of the older people will not have English as their first language. As a result, they may have difficulty not only in finding the appropriate words but also, because of cultural differences in styles of expression and education, not be able to convey concepts or precise meanings. Only an awareness of the limitations in communication can help one to listen with more patience and understanding.

Chapter 8 gives some information about major historical and social changes that help to give a background to the lives of the old people with whom one may wish to reminisce. An example of the value of such knowledge is the work of an occupational therapist in a day centre. When he was working with an old woman from Antigua in the Caribbean he found that he could not understand her unease in the tiny, rather gloomy room where they met. Once he had talked to her daughter however, he was able to understand how much of her early life had been spent in a community where the weather and custom meant that life was lived outdoors and so shared with neighbours and friends. Closed doors and walls meant not only the sunshine, but also friends, were excluded. The old woman had always planned to return home in time to die, but ill health and poverty were preventing her. Although the occupational therapist could not take her back to her home, he was able to respond more sensitively to what she was saying and to acknowledge her uneasiness. Learning more about her and her culture and about how life in England still felt different to her helped him to help her cope in the day centre and to ensure that she went outdoors whenever the sun shone. He reported this to the centre manager, so when the day centre was extended a sun lounge was built on for the benefit of this old woman and others like her.

Most literature about communication skills and counselling is still Euro-centric and is therefore of limited value in work with people from different cultures (Stewart, 1992). Watching and attempting to interpret body language, for example may be quite useless when talking to a old Chinese woman who will have almost certainly spent her life trying to keeping her face expressionless, unless this is understood. In many cultures it is considered quite improper to show or discuss emotions with strangers or those who have been known for just a little time. Physical touch, often used instinctively to give comfort, may also offend in some cultures, particularly if there are gender differences as well.

Perhaps the biggest pitfall in cross-cultural communication is the feeling in many white people that they are of superior intelligence to other races; it is not easy for people to rid themselves of this feeling even if they know that it is not true. If this attitude is compounded by a view that frail old people are not capable of making decisions for themselves, then there is a grave chance that their needs and wishes will be totally disregarded. It is essential that in any conversation with an old person, particularly if there is a cultural difference, that the helper's listening is not distorted by their own value system.

Mr Tyler's situation illustrates how age gaps can hinder understanding even when the listeners are from the same culture. He was an elderly dependent man who was admitted to a respite bed in a community hospital while his wife, who usually cared for him, underwent a minor operation. He was told that his wife was being moved to a hospital in another town. His distress at this news was out of all proportion to the message. Then his primary nurse realised that the distance to the neighbouring town, a mere 40 minutes' drive along a motorway to the car-owning professionals, brought back to the frail man memories of a full day's journey by bicycle as a youth, and to a town moreover, where opposing football teams had represented hostility to him. How then could he be content to hear of his wife, who was so important to him, being moved to this far-away alien place? Nothing but a fast and efficient journey in a voluntary worker's car and the sight of his wife in her new hospital bed reassured him.

Perhaps nothing separates the generations as much as attitudes towards intimate sexual behaviour, and this may make communication difficult. Young people, sensitive to changing patterns of the present day, may for example, in talking to old people ask about their 'partners' and risk bewildering if not offending them. Many old people will have had sexual partners to whom they were not married but their expectations of themselves and what they believe others have for them is that they had husbands and wives – partners are almost certainly something different to them. Equally confusing to relaxed and open communication is the view sometimes held by younger people of a narrow moral code in the early part of this century that was untransgressed by those who were young at that time. A group of care assistants admitted to each other that they had worked with quite a few old women before realising that these women were conveying with their bashful hints from 'I'd been a naughty girl' to 'Yes it was a quiet wedding'. They had been surprised and intrigued to realise that many of these old women had their first babies within four or five months of their marriage. Once they knew what was being hinted at, they could ask more open questions and some delightful, warm, and sometimes funny memories of days of courtship emerged.

Generalisations, as is well known, can be dangerous and time and care must be taken to see a very old person who may no longer be articulate as an individual. For example, Madie was a very distressed old woman who had spent most of her adult life in a close, loving relationship with another woman. After the death of her partner,

Madie had a breakdown and was eventually admitted to residential care from a psychiatric hospital. The care assistants, all women, needed to wash, dress and feed her and they could not understand her insistence that they must not come near her, or her distress when they had to do so. Madie was very ill and confused and it was never possible to know exactly what memories were stirred for her by this new imposed intimacy, but she seemed to express guilt and loss.

Confused old people are often able to reveal their fears even when they do not seem to be addressing them directly. John is 87 years old and calls his 20-year-old care assistant 'mother', often demanding to know why she has dumped him. He was 'dumped' in a children's home when he was ten years old. Now, 77 years later, the environment of the residential establishment and his sense of loss reminds him of that earlier intense pain. Learning about his background helped his care assistant to be tolerant of his anger and accusations and to comfort and reassure him when he acted like a hurt little boy.

When old people who are confused seem to talk nonsense it is important not to ignore them or to go along with their confusion. However strange their talk may seem, they are in touch with something that is real to them. For example, when a young primary nurse was bathing Jeannie, a woman very much older than herself, Jeannie kept on calling her 'Lily' and asked her not to be so rough with her. The nurse told her gently that her name was not Lily but Aleisha and then went on to ask 'Why? Do I remind you of Lily? Did Lily look like me? Was she Asian too?' Immediately the old woman became animated and, at the nurse's invitation, shared memories of Lily. She was an older girl, the daughter of a friend who had indeed been Asian and who had looked after her and her sisters when their young widowed mother had gone to work. Lily had been alternately kind and scolding, protective and harsh. From this spontaneous piece of reminiscence work a real bond was made between Jeannie and her nurse. The old woman seemed happier and her nurse was able to help her to accept the realities of life on the hospital ward.

Active listening of the kind that helped Jeannie is very rewarding although it sometimes takes courage to respond well. Loss or death can be frightening and difficult for a worker or relative to discuss with someone very old and sick. An exhausted old man who says 'I haven't long to go' almost certainly will want to talk about dying – his own death and who will be there at the time, who will miss him when he has gone, where he will be buried and how he would like to be remembered. It is tempting to ignore such a comment or to tell him that he is wrong but this will deny what he feels and knows to be true. What is undoubtedly true about old people is that they realise that they have not much longer to live and those who are young or younger assume that the old person finds this idea threatening. This must be true in some instances but many old people have a relaxed view that a long life must end; it is the loss of people with whom they share their days that makes them most distressed.

If enabling someone to talk about their death or the death of others who have been close to them, religious and cultural differences must be in our minds once more. The ways people feel about death and the practices that influence funerals and mourning are derived from religion and culture (Green and Green, 1991). An elderly Sikh man who believes in reincarnation is likely to have a totally different view of death from an irreligious English man. However, once again, it is important not to let cultural stereotypes hinder understanding: two Englishmen of the same age could, for example, have quite opposing views about Christianity and about burials and mourning rituals. One might expect to find many different views in the white native population of the British Isles.

It is possible to help old people face the end of life with acceptance, by seeing their place in the continuity or chain of events and people. It may help them to feel assured of continuity if they can be encouraged to discuss not only their children's or grandchildren's achievements but also to trace which of their own qualities or gifts they see reproduced in them. An old woman whose grandson is a well-known novelist needed to be encouraged to look at her own abilities; eventually, she was able to talk freely about herself as someone who loved books and telling stories and who had held her own children enthralled as they grew up. Simple questions will facilitate memories that help the old person to still feel significant. Who did your granddaughter get her lovely hair from? Who did your grandson get his brains from? Or who, in your family, had this kind of temperament?

Not all the people who need special care towards the end of their lives have had families. The solitary old person may of course have been a very lonely person all of their life but what did they do when they were alone? Perhaps they know a great deal about birds, perhaps they were gardeners, perhaps they are well-read and able to talk even now about books and ideas.

The pleasure in talking about oneself to an enthralled listener is certainly not confined to older people, indeed, it may well be the web that ensnares most lovers. However, the old people's stories may appear boring, repetitive or confused. When asked to comment on a present-day situation, old people can sometimes appear moralistic and punitive, but knowledge of the moral codes that conditioned their behaviour can make their attitudes more understandable. There are some attitudes, such as racism, that cannot be accepted however, and need addressing gently but persistently.

Pace of discussion with frail old people will be slow. The worker must be alert to physical problems that may have practical solutions: do they tire easily? are they comfortable? can they hear well enough?

if not, can they be seated differently? Do the practical arrangements ensure that the old person realises that a quiet time has been
set aside especially for them to talk about their past or to talk about
anything that bothers them or that they wish to share? Can they be
sure that there will be no interruptions, no eavesdroppers? The
listeners must be alert to what may be conveyed by someone too frail
to talk easily or too dependent to show anger openly. The old man
who falls asleep may not be able to stay awake or he may be closing
his eyes and conveying that he no longer wishes to talk. If the
old person wants the listener to go away then he or she must do
so. If they convey reluctance to talk because the interviewer is
intruding upon something that they do not wish to share, then
that person must be sensitive to this. If he or she is clumsy when
questioning and the old person conveys this, then they must apologise.

There is no doubt that, whatever the background of the old people,
for almost all of them communal living or being looked after by others
in day care or in their own homes will be a strange and alien
experience. There may be a few who during their working life have
worked in the armed forces and so have shared dormitories and large
dining rooms; there may be others who have grown up in institutions and have moved from one to the other, but for most people their
life experience will have been in a small house with their own family.
Living in a large institution surrounded by strangers or even living
in one's home but being looked after by many different people whom
one has not chosen would be frightening to anyone, let alone someone
who has lived so long they are now dependent upon others. It may
be possible, even at this stage, to help them to make new friends or
at least to feel at home in the group or valued and respected by
professional carers. Perhaps the most important way of doing this is
to reach their memories and to find occasions and happenings that
all of them have shared simply by living through the same period of
time. Almost certainly, in sharing, they will find that they have enjoyed
the same things, listened to the same songs, experienced some of the
same deprivations and achievements. Reminiscence, whether formal
or informal, plays a vital part in the sense of well-being for old
people. Skilful, thoughtful and sensitive communication is vital to its
success.

AN EXERCISE IN COMMUNICATION

In order to demonstrate to yourself what reminiscence feels like carry
out the following exercises working with someone with whom you
normally work but whom you do not know well.

Spend five minutes talking to your companion about
- your first day at school, or
- your first holiday, or
- your best friend when you were five years old.

Change around and allow your companion to tell you about the same thing. Then spend a little time sharing with each other what the experience was like. Were you surprised at how easily you remembered details or did they elude you? If the latter, what, if anything, brought them back? What emotions did you experience as you were talking? How do you feel now? Have your feelings about your fellow worker changed at all as a result of this shared discussion?

REFERENCES

Coleman, P.G. 1974. Measuring reminiscence characteristics. In *Int. Journal Aging Human Development*, **5**, 281–294.

Egan, G. 1990. *The Skilled Helper*, 4th edn. Brooks/Cole Publishing, Pacific Grove, California.

Green, J. and Green, M. 1991. *Dealing with Death, Practices and Procedures*. Chapman and Hall, London.

Havinghurst, R.G. and Glasser, R. 1972. An exploratory study of reminiscence. In *Journal of Gerontology*, **27**, 243–253.

Kiernat, J. 1979. The use of life review with confused nursing home residents. In *American Journal of Occupational Therapy*, **33**, 306–310.

Lazarus, L.W. 1976. A programme for the elderly at a private psychiatric hospital. In *Gerontologist*, **16**, 125–131.

Stewart, W. 1992. *A to Z of Counselling, Theory and Practice*. Chapman and Hall, London.

CHAPTER 4

Reminiscence with groups

Running a reminiscence group is an exciting and and immensely rewarding challenge; however, it can feel daunting, and in order to be successful it needs to be tackled in a systematic way. Before looking in detail at how to undertake reminiscence work with groups and developing a matrix which can be used to plan and monitor reminiscence group work, it is helpful to spend a little time looking at groups and group work in general. This will help with understanding what kinds of groups lend themselves to reminiscence work and something about group dynamics. The academic study of the sociology and social psychology of groups is extensive, but less has been written about group work practice. The approach to practice advocated in this chapter uses Heap's *Group Theory for Social Workers* (1977), a well-researched book that examines group work in a wide variety of settings and links it to theory and experimental work. Heap's book, Finlay's *Groupwork in Occupational Therapy* (1993) and Douglas's *Groupwork Practice* (1977) would be useful further reading.

Our whole lives are spent in groups of one sort or another, working, living or relaxing – groups in which we interact with other group members – although we do not usually think of life in these terms. In order to define what is meant by a group, one can take the example of a cinema audience who, although they technically constitute a group, do not feel like one. Why not? First, they sit in the dark and the opportunity to get to know the other people in the cinema does not exist. Second, all the seats face the same way making it awkward to interact with the other people. Third, the audience is large, and groups work best when they are small. Fourth, the satisfaction that people get from going to see a film relates to the film itself and not to being part of the group that forms the audience. Finally an individual only needs to be in the cinema watching the film to be satisfied, they do not have to participate in any other way. This analysis of the cinema audience demonstrates nicely that, in order to feel like a group, members must have the opportunity to get to know each other and interact with each other. The group must be small enough to let this happen, and group members need to get satisfaction from the activity they are undertaking as a member of that group and not just as an individual (Heap 1977). There is, however, no ideal group – group work involves working with members in order to create a balance within the group. Ways of achieving both this balance and group-determined goals are discussed later in this chapter.

TYPES OF GROUPS

Groups can be **psyche** or **socio**. **Psyche** groups exist to provide emotional satisfaction for their members and they tend to be informal, for example, the women who always sit together in the small lounge in a residential home, in order to be together. **Socio** groups come together to pursue specific goals, for example a reminiscence group. However, elements of socio groups exist within psyche groups and vice versa. The women in the small lounge also like to watch soap operas on television without being interrupted. A reminiscence group is deliberately structured to give group members emotional and personal satisfaction, in addition to pursuing the specific goal of reminiscing (Jennings, 1950).

Groups are commonly regarded as falling into three types, natural, formed or compulsory (Heap, 1977). Natural groups gravitate together of their own accord. Formed groups often occur in response to external pressure but members usually have the option of joining or not joining them. Compulsory groups come together because they must. They may be compelled by authority, for example members may be required by a court to attend a study group on alcohol abuse; or groups may be pseudo-voluntary – the head of home wants everyone to take part in a reminiscence or activity group and pressure is put on individuals to join. The compulsion may come from within the individuals themselves – they need to be a group member, perhaps because they are afraid of missing out or perhaps because they are jealous of Mrs Jones who has been asked to join. Although natural groups may reminisce, reminiscence groups are usually formed groups, having been brought together by a member of staff or a voluntary worker. Occasionally they may be compulsory groups. Try to avoid being put in the position of running a compulsory reminiscence group, as members of a compulsory group may not want either to be in the group or to pursue the group's specific goals. As a result reluctant group members can be disruptive, to the point of making it difficult for the group to function.

Reminiscence has its own gestalt, that is, reminiscence is more than the sum of its parts. Groups also develop a gestalt – a group mind – establishing what is acceptable to the group, and what is not. The group mind may be at variance with, or a modification of, what individual group members think. Group members may alter or suppress their views or beliefs in order to concur with the group's views. If they feel unable to do so they may withdraw from the group if they can, or they may become negative or disruptive if they cannot.

Groups in residential or hospital settings are open to special tensions as they are superimposed into the pre-existing groups that make up institutional living. When planning to run reminiscence groups in a home or hospital do give particular thought to what groups exist already. It may be helpful to read in more depth about work in residential settings. Brearley's *Residential Work with the Elderly* (1977) and Payne in McCaughan's *Group Work: Learning and Practice* (1978) are recommended.

THE GROUP LEADER'S ROLE

The worker initiating a reminiscence group is more than likely to end up as its leader and it is the leader's task to ensure that the group is functioning and achieving its goal(s). The leader must intervene when necessary but not dominate, and must help resolve difficulties in relationships within the group, and exercise control. Leadership requires enthusiasm and a genuine interest in the group and its members. It also requires the leader to be self-aware as this allows them to analyse both their own feelings and behaviour and what is happening within the group. It is helpful too for the leader to have some knowledge of the past and of the geography of different parts of Britain and the world. The information in Chapter 8 illustrates how varied people's backgrounds are. The dates and events also listed in that chapter provides a starting point for learning more about the past. A general knowledge is sufficient; the leader shouldn't get obsessed by historical knowledge and detail. If the group want to attribute the wrong date or place to an event, it does not really matter as the focus of reminiscence, unlike oral history, is on what group members say and feel about events. There may be no commonality of views amongst group members, which again does not matter providing that group members agree to differ, and sometimes the leader may need to spend time helping the group to do this.

The leader should spend time at the end of each session analysing both their own performance and how the group performed. Keeping notes of this will provide a record of the group's development and progress and help with developing leadership skills by giving the opportunity to reflect on past performances. These notes will also be useful when approaching the task of setting up groups in the future. People new to reminiscence group work will find it helpful to run a group with a co-worker. Co-workers can offer each other support in addition to evaluating each other's performances and exploring what is happening in the group both in terms of its dynamics and in terms of how well it is doing in achieving its tasks.

PLANNING AND RUNNING A GROUP

I keep six honest serving men
(They taught me all I know)
Their names are WHAT and WHY and WHEN
and HOW and WHERE and WHO
        'The Elephant's Child' in *The Just So Stories*
                     by Rudyard Kipling

In addition to this quotation being an exercise in happy reminiscence for one of the authors, it does provide a useful and easy-to-remember matrix or set of headings against which to design, build and evaluate a reminiscence group, for when planning a group, one needs to consider a number of issues from a number of angles.

The 'Why'

Start by writing down the reasons for running a group: the 'why' or 'whys'. Reasons for running a group may include giving particular people pleasure be they patients, clients or staff fostering new relationships between group members and boosting individual group members' confidence to help them redevelop social skills that they have lost because they have become depressed or isolated. In addition it may be that the worker initiating the group would like the chance to develop group leadership skills. Perhaps the reason could be to provide material for a display at the local library, or an essay or a project. It is worth taking time over establishing the why or whys and ensuring that everyone's reasons are covered, including those of the workers involved. Workers in the caring professions tend not to acknowledge their own personal needs; by not doing so they run the danger of creating hidden personal agendas that can damage or subvert a group. At this stage the list of whys will be private to the worker[s] initiating the group. The private list of whys could look something like this:

- Our senior manager Mrs Ward wants our centre to start some new activities.
- We have two new women who have joined the centre in the last month and they have not settled in easily.
- Mrs Moon and Mrs White both have very poor short-term memories which seem to make them very anxious and demanding of staff, and staff find this a nuisance at times.
- I want to develop my skills and to enhance my career prospects; group work is something I have never done.
- I would like to try group work but I want to try it with people with whom I feel safe.

So I would like to include:

- Mrs Raju because I like her and she likes me and she can be very sociable given the chance; but being in a wheelchair and unable to propel herself makes being sociable difficult for her and I sometimes feel that our day care people exclude her because she is Indian.
- Mr Brown, because he is a dear and often misses out because he is blind.
- Annie, one of the care assistants, because she is interested in the past and collects antique bits and pieces.

Next prioritise this private list of reasons and develop a public statement of the reasons for establishing a reminiscence group, which might look something like this:

- Mrs Ward our senior manager has asked us to start some new activities at the centre.
- I would like to start a group that would share our memories and talk about the past. I have never run a group before but I would like to try.
- I would like to involve Annie the care assistant who is very interested in the past and who collects bits and pieces of memorabilia.
- I would also like to ask Mr Brown, Mrs Raju, Mrs Moon and Mrs White because I feel they would enjoy it and benefit from spending time in a small group.
- And I would like to include Mrs Read and Miss Green because they are new here.

Share this public statement with anyone who has or might have a vested interest in the group, in particular with potential group members, doing this as you approach them to ask if they would like to join the group and then later with the group in its first session. At the first session it may be necessary to add to or alter the list in the light of what group members say. This list will form the basis of the group's contract, a contract to which members jointly agree to work and against which the performance of the group can be monitored.

The 'Who'

The 'Who' includes people who will actually belong to the group as well as the people in the wider context in which the group takes place. People who can influence the group's development, in other words, those who can help with making a success of things and, conversely, have the potential to cause problems are also included in the 'who'.

Who should be in the group?

Size is important: six to eight people is the best size for a group. Above ten is too large and some people will not be able to fully participate, or even at all. If there are blind, deaf or demented people in the group keep it very small. The interests of some very impaired people might be better served by one-to-one work. The membership will be determined to an extent by the list of reasons. The preceding sample list gave six people who would benefit from being in a small group for a variety of reasons. Two had poor short-term memories: being in a group where they could use their long-term memories could help them become less anxious and demanding. Two were new to the centre and had not integrated. Two the group leader liked and knew, giving the leader support and confidence and also they were isolated. Annie had something to offer to a reminiscence group and to offer to the leader.

When approaching people to see if they would like to join the group it is important to do this in a way that gives them the option of not joining if they do not want to. The intention is to establish a formed group not a compulsory one. An explanation of the public statement of whys should be accompanied by asking if there is anything they would want to add. They may have suggestions about who they would like to see in the group. They may want time to think about the whole idea before making a commitment. When approaching people remember Coleman's significant minority of old people who were troubled by talking about the past, saw no point in doing so, or could not bear to do so (Coleman, 1989). Listen to what people say, and if they are a member of that significant minority do not coerce them, whatever the pressures are to do so. They will not benefit and nor will the group.

As shown in Chapter 3, it is not always easy to hear what people are actively saying. This is particularly true of demented or confused people and it is very easy to whisk someone in a wheelchair into a situation in which they do not want to be. If after the first session or two it is obvious that a particular person is not comfortable in the group give them the opportunity to leave. They may need time privately to discuss what went wrong or they may want to forget the whole episode or indeed appear to do so. Make sure that it is recorded that this is someone who does not feel comfortable either with reminiscence or with that particular group of people, so that they are not put through the experience a second time.

Group members often develop what is called 'group bond' (Heap, 1977). This is the 'we' feeling: that the group is not only a useful place to be, but it is also a good place to be, a place where people feel they belong. Group members differentiate themselves from non-members as a result of this. This sense of belonging is particularly important to people who do not feel they fit or belong elsewhere. The leader must ensure that the sense of belonging helps group members in the rest of their lives and does not hinder them by creating an over-dependence on the group. An over-dependence could make living in a residential home or on a ward, or communicating with other people, more difficult for them than it already is.

Groups ascribe particular roles to their members. Almost every group has a clown, and when groups are comfortable and functioning well clowns are appreciated and enjoyed, but if the going gets tough the clown may no longer be appreciated. If the group member who is playing the clown continues to act as a clown because they cope with life in general in this way and know no other way of behaving, the group leader may need to support and protect the clown. Try saying something like, 'It is sometimes easier to laugh than to cry and I am sure that John would not want you to feel that he made a joke about something so sad'. The role of scapegoat is a common one occurring in almost all groups at one time or another (Douglas, 1978). Clowns who cannot adapt and others whose behaviour is deemed inappropriate or unacceptable by the group may become scapegoats. Or the scapegoat may be a confused or disoriented member of the group, perhaps someone who tells the same story over and over again. In this case the group may scapegoat them for making a session boring, or the group dull. Scapegoating is difficult to deal with and it may be necessary to bring it out into the open by saying something like 'I think we are all responsible in one way or another for today's session not going so well and it really is not fair to blame Mollie'.

There may also be someone in the group whose strength may pose a threat to the authority of the group leader. This kind of situation cannot be resolved without involving the group perhaps by saying something like 'As you know, I was the person who brought us all together and helped us to agree what we wanted to do and to start doing it. I think that is something that Jack would like to do now on behalf of the group and perhaps we can talk about that'. In the event it is extremely unlikely, given the nature of people who make up reminiscence groups, that the group will endorse Jack as their new leader, but a leader's position in the group depends on their position being sanctioned by the group (Heap, 1977).

If there is someone extremely interesting in the group, it is important not to abandon the principles of running a reminiscence group and concentrate solely on that person. Perhaps they are someone who could contribute separately to an oral history in addition to being part of the reminiscence group.

Who – the wider context

Running a group can be a lonely and anxious business at times but it can also be a very rewarding one. In any event the group leader is going to need all the help and support they can get including help to ensure that obstacles are not thrown in the way or that attempts, albeit unintentionally, are made to sabotage the group. Work out on paper a 'map' of the dynamics of the centre, home or place where the groups meets. Who is the manager or person in charge? The person in authority will need to know about the plans for the group and to give their permission for, and ideally their support to, the group. In the example given, Mrs Ward the senior manager ought to prove an ally – after all it was her idea – but the group leader needs to ensure that Mrs Ward knows how she could give help and support. Someone outside the immediate setting could also be very helpful to the group's success by supporting and sanctioning it. They could give the idea of running a reminiscence group a status which it might not otherwise have. Someone working in a local authority-run day centre might find that an interested district or county councillor or an interested middle-manager could be a great ally. In a hospital setting it might be an enthusiastic consultant or registrar.

Sources of help and support exist in surprising places. Share the reasons for wanting to establish a group with a wide range of people; more often than not this will result in people coming forward who are prepared to help. They may offer to help in a variety of ways, for example by providing material, or perhaps by playing the piano, or explaining the benefits of the group to others.

If it is proving difficult to map out the context in which the group will take place or if the people in that wider context are being negative or obstructive it might help to do some reading and thinking about the kinds of groups that make up complex organisations and their relationships with one another. Heap has a good chapter on groups in traditional organisations. Although an old text, Goffman's book *Asylums: Essays on the Social Situation of Mental Patients and Others* (1960), has a stark simplicity in its explanations that still make a useful contribution to the understanding of people and their place within traditional monolithic organisations.

The 'What'

Addressing the 'what' basically means giving the group a structure. Being in a group can feel strange, dangerous and frightening. In order to work properly the group needs to feel safe and the leader does too. When the group agrees its contract it also agrees what its agenda should be, both the contract and the agenda being based on the public statement of 'whys'. Items for the group's agenda fall into three areas. First, what are the group's tasks to be? For example, does it want to work towards a display or presentation for the rest of the centre? Or does it want to be a purely social group? The answers to these questions may not all come at once. It is important to keep seeking answers in order to ensure that the group members are clear about their agreed tasks; if they decide to change to a different task or tasks they do so by agreement and not by default. Second, decide how many sessions the group will run for. Stick to the agreed number of sessions. This is much less easy than it sounds: if a group is going well there is a temptation to let it drift on and meet week after week. The importance of endings is addressed later in this chapter. In order to keep to the agreement the leader may have to confront the temptation to drift by saying something like 'We agreed that this group would only run for six sessions and we have now come to the end of our six sessions. However, we can discuss whether or not we want to set up another group and think about what that group could do, and who from this group would like to be in it'. Usually six or eight sessions of one-and-a-half hours is about right. Open-ended drop-in groups do work in some settings and for some tasks; however, what a reminiscence group is doing is bringing together vulnerable people who either have little recent experience of being in an interactive group or who have lost some of their social skills and need a structure within which they can develop their confidence. So if the group knows that it is meeting for an hour once a week for six weeks and then reviewing the situation at the end of that time, members will be more relaxed and get more out of the experience.

Third, decide the structure of the sessions. An overall structure needs setting at the beginning and a detailed structure for each session can be agreed at the end of the previous session. The group may want the leader to structure the sessions on its behalf; this however should be agreed by the group and not assumed by the leader. Each session should be resourced properly, by borrowing objects or by asking group members to bring objects in, by using music or poetry, or by preparing themes for discussion. When thinking about resources remember that the group members themselves are resources and are readily available. Age Exchange's *Practical Guide to Reminiscence Work* (1986) usefully suggests seven broad themes: childhood, at school, the neighbourhood, helping the adults, special occasions and special places, growing-up years, adult life. A group may want to focus on a different theme each week or to spend more than one session on each theme. If it is possible, end each session with a cup of tea which rounds things off and gives people time to move mentally out of the group and back into everyday life. Also people may be thirsty after all that talking!

The 'Where'

The Meeting Room

It is important to find somewhere that is friendly and as neutral as possible, in other words, a room that does not carry any bad memories or reminders of traumatic experiences for people. That may sound dramatic but it is well illustrated by a reminiscence group where the residential worker who was leading the group carefully chose the visitors' room in the home because it was cosy, central and well soundproofed. The first couple of sessions felt good and worked well. But she had forgotten that the room was also used for case conferences and for crisis meetings. It was at the end of the third session that Harry stayed behind to tell his story. It had been in that room that he and his wife had agreed to emergency admission to the home: he was blind and, because of her rapidly failing health, she could no longer care for him. Soon after, she deteriorated further, was admitted to hospital, and died whilst he remained in the home. It had been in that room that Harry was told that she had died. Clearly this is a very dramatic example of how even the best of rooms chosen with the best of motives could turn out to have sinister aspects for someone. The story has a more reassuring ending: Harry, having revealed his unease and been asked if he felt it would be helpful to him if the group moved, said that it was helping him to come to terms with his loss by joining the group, and that he felt alright about meeting in the room and in the home where recently a series of tragic events had changed his life forever.

Seating arrangements

Seating arrangements are extremely important. The group leader should use their knowledge of group members when drawing up a proposed seating plan taking account of people's physical needs, their hearing and sight abilities, the need for wheelchairs and other requirements. For example, if anyone might need the lavatory urgently, they will need to be near the door. They should also take account of people's personalities and their ability to contribute to the group.

Heap (1977) and Douglas (1978) both quote research that confirms that sitting in a circle is best as communication works both across and around. Within the circle some seats will allow easy communication with others. Demonstrate this by drawing a circle and an isosceles triangle within that circle ensuring that the triangle's points touch the circle. It is the seats at those points that communicate best with each other. The group leader might decide to put a withdrawn or tentative person in such a seating relationship with a dominant group member or with themselves. Avoid having dominant group members in this seating relationship as this will make it difficult for anyone else to get a look in. Also avoid having two articulate or strong characters sitting side-by-side; the temptation will be for them to communicate directly with each other and this will disadvantage other group members. It is extremely helpful to draw a diagram after each group session of both the seating arrangements and how interactions took place. This is an excellent way to learn about group dynamics and practical methods of managing them. One simple management technique is for the leader to change their seat within the group during a session in order to right a wrong balance, or to support a scapegoat or a weak or disadvantaged group member. Another is to ensure that people sit in a better configuration in the next session.

The 'When'

Jot down a timetable for the home, ward or centre to see when the best time will be to run a group. A bad atmosphere can be created because colleagues feel that the group leader has gone off to 'have a nice time with their group' when everyone is short-staffed. Equally, it is important to choose a time of day when the group is least likely to be interrupted by people who need to provide essential services to group members such as injections or dressings. If the group wants to meet after lunch is it likely that everybody will be asleep? There are no right or wrong answers. Many groups have failed dismally after lunch, as most of the members fell asleep, but they can succeed. One Head of Home who started a series of activities entitled 'Is There Life After Lunch? Clubs' included a very successful lively reminiscence group. If the time of day is clearly wrong, talk about it in the group and see if it can be changed. If it cannot, discuss the reasons why and reach a decision about how best to cope with the difficulties or distractions.

The 'How'

It is not possible to walk into a group and run it unprepared –
preparation is essential. Often, group work entails more work before
starting the group and after it finishes than actually during the sessions
themselves. Preparation includes work described in this chapter:
deciding the reasons why the group is meeting as a group; who is
going to be in the group and who in the system can help; where the
group is to meet and the ramifications of that choice; the structure,
that is, what the group is going to do; when, how often, and for how
long the group is going to meet. Check before each session that everything is covered and that the group is still able to fulfil its contract.
If it is feeling that it cannot do so raise this with the group and decide
whether to change the contract and make a new one or whether the
original contract can be renegotiated.

Both the leader and group members need to be physically and
mentally prepared for the session. Group members may need help
with toileting prior to the meeting so that they do not need to disturb
the session. Being prepared mentally is important too. One worker
learned this the hard way by rushing into a group a couple of minutes
late with a head full of other things and finding that it took a long
time to come down to earth and become part of the group. This is
not acceptable. If it does ever happen, apologise to the group, explain
and ask for two or three minutes to clear your head and then start
the group session properly, and perhaps finish the appropriate number
of minutes late.

The way in which the group communicates will determine how it
works and one of the leader's tasks is to ensure that everybody has
an equal opportunity to contribute to the group if they wish to. People
communicate for a range of reasons. It may be to give and receive
instruction and information – 'No, you spat on the flat iron like that
to see if it was hot enough'. Some may wish to impart experiences
and reactions – 'When we got on board the SS *Windrush* to come to
Britain, my knees went like jelly and I had to sit down. It wasn't just
the ship's engines and the movement of the water, you know, I
suddenly thought to myself, Hettie are you doing the right thing here?'
Or they may want to elicit responses and clarify messages – 'You
remember don't you Doris when we children were all asked to that
party at the town hall?' or 'I wasn't talking about rationing during
the war, I was talking about 1952, that was years after the war had
ended.' Group members will demonstrate attitudes and opinions –
'I don't know about young people today. My neighbour's niece has
bought a flat with her boyfriend and they have moved in there
together, right out in the open. In our day you waited and did it
properly. Bert and I were walking out for five years and engaged for

four before we had enough money to put down on a home, and then we got married.' Or they may try to influence others, using words or non-verbal gestures and body language – May winking at Doris before leaning back and closing her eyes as Mrs Taylor tells the story about how her father became a policeman for the umpteenth time. People also use sounds to give words emphasis and eye contact to give meaning emphasis and when making critical points or ending interaction, although eye contact rarely lasts for more than a second or so (Argyle and Dean, 1965).

> Olive, who had worked as a hairdresser, could no longer contain herself. 'You held the curling tongs like *this*' she almost shouted at Mrs Bryan, looking her straight in the eye.

Communication has been described as 'overt and manifest' or 'covert and latent' (Heap, 1977). Overt and manifest communication is straightforward; body language and words all give the same message. For example, 'Joan sat up straight and looked me in the eye. "I'd love to join your reminiscence group", she said firmly'. If, however, Joan's communication was covert or latent, the interchange could go something like this:

> Joan remained slumped in her chair with her eyes closed. 'I once went to one of those sort of groups, it was all right,' she said. I reached for her hand and held it. 'Do you want to come to this one?' I asked. 'All right, I don't mind if I do,' she replied in a monotone. However, whilst speaking she squeezed my hand in a way that suggested that she really did want to join the group, something that her words, the sound she made and her body language had not communicated.

Covert or latent communication gives mixed messages which can take some decoding. Some people will give mixed messages because of their physical or mental impairments, for example, someone who has speech difficulties and cries easily because of a stroke that has left them emotionally labile.

Bales (1970) describes three interactive aspects of communication: social emotional negative, social emotional positive and task area. Weighting in either of the first two had a clear impact on the third, either blocking or enhancing progress towards achieving the group's tasks. In other words, the ability of the group to achieve its task is affected by whether it is feeling socially or emotionally positive or negative. It is useful to analyse both good and difficult sessions or parts of sessions using Bales' theory. This analysis will demonstrate how the climate in the group is affected by its members. It also gives the leader the opportunity to consider how to influence communication in order to enhance the group. If a sub-group alliance forms within the group, this can disrupt the life and progress of the group. Groups are powerful and people may feel the need to form such alliances in order to defend themselves both against other individuals in the group and against the group itself or its chosen task. Such self-defence can take active or passive forms. On the one hand, it could be a verbal attack on the group or leaving the room, on the other silence, closed eyes or even sleep. Do not let such behaviour pass; find out what has caused it, analyse what has happened using Bales' theory and then either explore it with the group or, if it is more appropriate, talk privately with the person concerned.

Endings

It is important to spend time thinking about the final session of the group. Endings are difficult. This needs to be accepted before starting to look at how to manage an ending and saying goodbye. At the end of the group's life people need to say goodbye to the group and to each other. They may want to do this by going round and allowing each individual to say, formally, how they felt about the group, or they may prefer to say goodbye spontaneously. The latter usually works better as it allows everyone to contribute what they feel like in their own time.

Imagine five weeks have passed and the group agreed to meet for six weeks. If it has gone well people will probably employ a range of tactics to avoid facing up to ending the group: 'Did you say six weeks? I don't remember that at all.' 'For the week after next [what would have been week 7] I've asked my daughter to let me have that christening robe I told you about.' 'I thought you [the group leader] were enjoying the group; I didn't realise you didn't want to carry on.' The natural and very understandable reaction in the face of these comments is to allow the group to continue to meet without a contract. It is important not to do this, for a number of reasons.

First, the members of the group made a commitment and a contract to meet for a specified length of time. It was a new venture for everyone and in order to feel secure everyone needed to be certain of each other and of what was expected of them as individuals. Now the group has come to the end of that commitment. It is therefore the group that needs to decide whether or not to make a further commitment and, if so, what that commitment should be. A new beginning requires a fresh commitment and a new contract. This will allow people to feel safe as they know what they are committing themselves to and what is expected of them.

Second, group members must be allowed to decide for themselves what they want to do next. Usually everyone has an opinion, although some people will need more help and support than others in making their opinion known. Groups never fail to surprise. One group who had thoroughly enjoyed using artifacts and old household objects said, 'Forget the old glass bottles and the like, they were interesting but what we want to do next is to have a current affairs discussion group and we will club together to buy the newspapers to resource it.' Another group may want to continue reminiscence but to work towards providing their childhood memories for children at a local primary school. In one instance in which this happened, the group leader and a class teacher were able to arrange for the group of old people and a primary school class to write letters to each other about their current lives. The old people also wrote about their childhoods.

Third, reviewing the group's contract creates the opportunity for change, for new people, both old people and members of staff and volunteers, to try reminiscence, and allows people who want to opt out of the group to do so.

Fourth, it is an opportunity for the group to affirm itself. This means saying out loud, 'Together we have achieved something special; we are not going to dilute that experience by pretending we have not come to the end of our sessions; what we are going to do is take away with us that specialness.' It is very moving and rewarding to see people who, prior to being in a reminiscence group, had lost both the confidence and social skills to chat or mix, using the specialness the group has given them to do just that, not only within the group but also elsewhere.

Finally, goodbyes and good endings are very important. The theories of life review and life validation, cited in Chapter 5, demonstrate how important it is for people to revisit past conflicts and crises in order to address and hopefully resolve them, so that they can feel fully valued and valid. Many old people are vulnerable because of previous life events and the emotional luggage and physical legacy these events have left them with, including incomplete or unsaid goodbyes. In a safe secure group an opportunity exists, maybe for the first time, for people to say goodbye properly and to end something special, their group membership. They can reflect on the good bits, talk about the bits they did not like or found difficult in the group, and demonstrate to themselves that they can not only survive endings but that they can also draw strength from doing this. This may be traumatic and painful for some people as it may stir up buried memories of unsaid goodbyes or endings that went wrong.

Groups have the strength within themselves to help and support group members who are upset. The group leader may need to unlock that strength by allowing a silence to run for a bit, and then by saying something like: 'What Lily has just said has I am sure struck a deep chord with all of us – do we want to sit and think about it or does anyone want to talk about it?' It is important that after allowing the group time to explore what Lily has raised, to bring things together and set them back safely and securely in the context of the present and the group by summarising the group's experience: 'We have had six weeks of meeting as a group, six weeks in which we have shared a lot of things, we have laughed a lot and we have cried and we have said what we want to do next is [describe your arrangements and agreement]. We are all going to take away from the group something special including special feelings about each other.' Often at the end of the final session people will hug and kiss and say goodbye as if they were leaving the area.

SUMMARY

By running a reminiscence group one can give particular people personally and socially rewarding experiences, by fostering new relationships between group members, boosting individuals' confidence and helping them redevelop social skills that they have lost. Given the nature of the members of a reminiscence group and the way in which a group functions, the quality of the experience that it produces for its members will depend heavily on the ability of the group leader to plan and manage. Ability grows with practice, supported by the careful analysis of current and past experiences. Leading a reminiscence group or being part of one is a powerful, rewarding and challenging experience. The positive quality of that experience is at odds with much of the research literature which is inconclusive about the value of reminiscence. What it is not at odds with is the feelings of people who have been part of successful reminiscence groups: their advice and that of the authors is to join a group or set one up and find out for yourself.

REFERENCES

Age Exchange. 1986. *Practical Guide to Reminiscence Work*. Age Exchange, London.

Argyle, M. and Dean, J. 1965. Eye contact distance and affiliation. In *Sociometry*, **28**, 289–304.

Bales, R.F. 1970. *Personality and Interpersonal Behaviour*. Holt, Rinehart and Winston, New York.

Brearley, P. 1977. *Residential Work with the Elderly*. Routledge and Kegan Paul, London.

Coleman, P. 1989. *Ageing and Reminiscence Processes: Social and Clinical Implications*. John Wiley and Sons, Chichester.

Douglas, T. 1977. *Groupwork Practice*. Tavistock, London.

Finlay, L. 1993. *Groupwork and Occupational Therapy*. Chapman and Hall, London.

Goffman, E. 1960. *Asylums: Essays on the Social Situation of Mental Patients and Others*. Penguin, Harmondsworth.

Heap, K. 1977. *Group Theory for Social Workers*. Pergamon.

Jennings, H.H. 1950. *Leadership and Isolation*, 2nd edn. Longmans and Green, New York.

McCaughan, N., ed. 1978. *Group Work: Learning and Practice*. George Allen and Unwin.

CHAPTER 5

Life reviews and
life history books

There is great value in helping old people to review their lives. In this
chapter the ways and means of doing so are considered in more detail.
It includes suggestions for making life history books with old people
as a means of providing an interesting and easily accessible record
of their achievements.

THE VALUE OF LIFE REVIEWS

It has been suggested that the wish and the need to review one's life
is well nigh universal and that it is essential to the task of facing up
to the end of life and reaching a sense of completeness and satisfaction
about all that one has done (Butler, 1963). However, Peter Coleman
challenges this idea; he acknowledges the value of reminiscence and
life reviews but considers that not everyone benefits from them and
cautions that one needs to test out the individual's satisfaction with
their life before engaging them formally in reflecting on the past
(Coleman, 1989). Both Butler and Coleman in common with other
writers on this subject, for example Norris (1987) and Kiernat (1979),
acknowledge the evident pleasure and benefit to the mood of the old
people that sharing reminiscence brings. What also seems to be clear
is that if one is to relate to an old person who cannot talk freely about
the present and who does not have much future to speculate about,
one has to use their memories in order to give them comfort and
understand their concerns.

Just as reminiscing is a familiar activity so too is the practice of
reflecting upon the past in order to make sense of the here and now
and to understand the influences that have shaped it. Whenever an
important decision has to be made about one's lifestyle, a change of
career for example, or a more threatening crisis, most people make

the decision after looking back to find evidence that they can cope, by reflecting on the things that they have achieved so far and thus gaining some confidence that they can develop new skills and manage the changes. When making this kind of evaluation there is usually a chance to talk with a friend or partner about it and with them reach an honest and helpful view of what is required. People facing a crisis alone or whose partners are no longer able to help them may need the intervention of a professional worker – most people in extreme old age fall into this group. The workers best placed to help the old people to review their lives are those who care for their daily needs, that is, residential workers, staff from nursing homes, day centres, domiciliary care or hospitals, also friends, relatives, or indeed anyone who visits isolated old people in their homes. The number of old people cared for in the community will increase with the changing shape of the population and community care legislation and many more younger helpers, including family members, could become involved in this work.

It is not always easy to undertake such work. It can be disturbing to learn, for example, that a mentally frail old man who requires help with the most commonplace and personal tasks has once run his own garage business, has been headmaster of a local school or had a golf handicap of 18. The helpers will almost certainly become closer to the old people while reviewing their lives with them and so become more distressed by their frailty or impending death. The vulnerability and losses of extreme old age are probably threatening to everyone, and it is not possible to escape noting them when they are to be measured against the achievements of the younger person now grown old and weak. The threat is greater for carers who may themselves be at or past middle age or for anyone who has members of his own circle, family or friends, who are very old or who have recently died. If carers are to be encouraged to work in this way with very old people and thus expose themselves to some distress, then managers or colleagues working in this field must be aware that some support and time will be needed for them to talk about their feelings. There is little doubt that the sense of doing an important job, of being close to old people and of making the quality of life in their last few years immensely richer, will bring much satisfaction to them. However, there will be times when they are truly sad, such as after the death of a special person when they feel they have lost someone close to them, as indeed they will have done. If a climate can be developed that acknowledges this sadness and provides time, space and support for staff to discuss their involvement and their feelings, then everyone, including the old people, will benefit. Some groups set up especially to support family carers already offer this kind of help and it is important that they continue to do so.

Nevertheless, as Butler's research shows (1963), preparing a life history is important and can be a genuine comfort to a very old person. The task of working with someone to review details of their life is in itself a healing process and evidence of interest and respect; if these details are written down then the record itself prevents the nature and quality of the individual from being forgotten. The record can provoke genuine interest and be the focus for enquiry and discussion between the professional carer and the elderly person and a source of joy and discovery to grandchildren and other family members. If carers, whether relatives, professionals, friends or neighbours, decide that it would benefit an old person to be engaged in a life review then they need to decide whether to do this in a structured way and set time aside each day for quiet work with them or to simply use opportunities as they occur in ordinary contact or discussion. There is no exemplar for this work but it is essential that the carers hold in their minds the aims of the discussions and with respect and patience demonstrate that they have heard what the old person wants to tell them and with gentle questioning encourage them to comment on their own achievements.

Work with a person near the end of life is valuable in itself, however the value may be lessened in the long term if the old person has a poor short-term memory and cannot remember the conversation from one day to the next, or even one hour to the next. Moreover the worker will not always be on hand and if he or she knows important facts about the old person that are not known to others then the old person may not be perceived or handled consistently. For these reasons therefore making a life history book, that is a written record of the significant facts about the lives of individuals, is advocated. A life history book is valuable not only because in its preparation the old person is able to reflect and validate his life, and time and attention is given to him to do so but also because once the record is made it remains as a document for the interest of the subject and also gives powerful messages to professional and family carers about the older person who may no longer be able to do so for himself.

It is wrong to assume that a person whose short-term memory is poor or who seems withdrawn will not be able to reminisce nor get great satisfaction from doing so. However, Coleman's research (1989) is a reminder to check with the elderly person that he or she wants to talk and to be alert for fatigue or unrelenting sadness. Joe, whose story follows, was someone who seemed totally turned into himself before he started to talk about Bess. Joe was a very sick man who talked for along time about his wife giving all sorts of homely details about her. He was over 75 years old and still grieved about the loss of his dear Bess who had died twenty years before. He seemed young again when he described how she looked and how he loved her long 'mousey-brown' hair. He told of the bread that she baked every Monday, leaving the dough to rise while she got on with the washing and how he remembered the mingled smells of baking bread and soap when he got home from work. In the parcel of personal belongings that he brought from his own house there was a faded black and white photograph of Bess, who looked rather stout and peevish; Joe however was delighted. Bess's photograph brought back many memories and he insisted that it went alongside his written description of her as an illustration. In spite of the loving way that he recalled details of many years previous, he could not remember what he had had for his tea even a short time after finishing eating.

Whatever approach is taken to helping old people to review their lives it is essential that they are helped to make an assessment of their lives free of other people's values obscuring the process. It may be easier, for example, to be impressed by someone who was a successful businessman who knew many famous people and to encourage him to talk about them, but it may require more persistence to encourage a lifelong factory worker to recall the pleasure and pride that he felt, perhaps about his exemplary timekeeping and the friendship that he earned among his fellow workers. A balanced view is possibly even more important if the old person is expressing regret, when very careful and sensitive listening is required. An old woman may want to tell us about her disappointment at not having had children which will probably have been a cause of tension for her for a large part of her adult life and she may wish to talk about the hopes and then the disappointments that each month brought. The worker will need to give her time to tell of these things and acknowledge her feelings; then, when she is ready, move her on to remember how she did express her loving and caring nature. She may well have 'mothered' the children of the entire neighbourhood, taken to looking after animals or known a particularly close relationship with her husband where the roles of lover, spouse and mother were combined.

LIFE HISTORY BOOKS

A life history book can be as long or as short as the subject wishes to make it. It cannot, of course, be a detailed record of his or her life but what must be recorded are those things that the subject wishes to include. Most life history books are no more than 10–12 pages including photographs and usually record the significant details: place and date of birth, family members, school, education and employment, adulthood and marriage, married life, children and grandchildren. However, if a life history book were to include only such details it would probably not be very interesting; it is the comment, the individual's wry evaluation of his or her achievements that make these records unique and give them their personal value. Though it may include reference to events of national or international significance, the focus of the life history book is on the old person,and how he or she felt *about* the events, not on the events themselves.

A life history book is, in effect, a conversation systematically recorded with the subject of the book having the power to decide what will or will not be included. It is their property once it has been written and while they are able to do so they will decide who will see it. Nevertheless it has to be borne in mind that the old person may become too frail to guard it and so its contents should take into account the possibility that many people may see it. If it has to be given into the safekeeping of someone else, for example a staff member, its value should be stressed and they should be asked to ensure that time is made to read it to or with the old person. Too many opportunities for giving comfort and delight will be lost if the life history book is felt by staff to be so precious that it ends up locked in an office drawer.

The person making the recording must keep on verifying with the very old person that the facts are recorded correctly and that names and places are spelt properly; otherwise they may be offended or even confused. One old woman was caused some amusement and not a little anger when the name of her village was at first misspelt and then the name of a large town given instead. Photographs add particular interest to a book and they are nearly always available. So often photographs lie at the bottom of drawers, rarely looked at by family members, and in many instances discarded when homes and their contents are emptied and sold off. If they are included in the life history book they become a very accessible form of comfort to the older person. Photographs and details of places and events known to older people can usually be obtained from museums, libraries and newspaper offices; these can stimulate an old person's memory as well as being a source of delight if included in the record.

Although a care manager, social worker, nurse, residential worker or care assistant is often best placed to work with a client in writing their life history, any concerned or sensitive person can do so. Some of the most valuable and powerful books have been written by the children of ageing parents. When the old person has had the strength to do so, sharing the task has helped the move to a nursing home or hospice and away from the family to be a loving and positive change. Written records can keep alive links between old people and their partners, families and friends. If the old person comes from an ethnic or religious minority group and is likely to be looked after in their new life by people who have no knowledge of their religion or culture then the record may be the most important means of ensuring that his or her needs and wishes are taken into account.

The first task of preparing a life history book is to be sure that the subject knows that it is a record for their own use and that its value is to record, at a time when they may be frail or forgetful, their achievements. A record of their lives is important because they are important; few people find this idea threatening, most are rather thrilled at it. It is possible to introduce the idea by saying something like 'You know we have had many conversations and you have told me a lot of interesting things about yourself. Do you think it would be a good idea if we wrote this down so there it would be a record forever? Your children or grandchildren might like to see it. Would it be nice for you, when you sit here quietly, to read about all those things that you have told me?'

Next, the worker and the old person must decide who is to make the book and how the recording is to be made. Occasionally the subject completes the practical work on their own book. A Macmillan nurse, for example, worked with a woman who was terminally ill and she herself chose to write down the story of her life. The nurse's task was to encourage her to do so and to help her to reflect, evaluate, grieve and to take comfort from her life thus far. Many elderly people will find the recording tiring and it may need to be done for them. However, they must be consulted as to what they want recorded and how they want it to be done. Large scrapbooks, with clear bold handwritten notes interspersed with photographs, tend to make the most attractive presentations but typewritten bound papers also serve. For those people whose sight is no longer good, an audio recording is invaluable. An audio recording can of course be illustrated with music or speeches recorded by others. An example of such an illustration is of the song 'Alice Blue Gown' that was included in a by then very old Alice's history. She also included the opening sentences of the abdication speech by Edward VIII because Alice, who always fancied that she looked a little like Mrs Simpson, remembered weeping for the lovers when she heard that the king was giving up his throne in order to marry Mrs Simpson. Finding the appropriate recording or historical detail can take time but librarians or members of local history societies can be a great source of help and once they know why the search is being made they are likely to be enthralled and give their time freely.

It takes time to prepare a life history book and it may be necessary to agree with the old person that a set period of time will be set aside every week, say one hour every other day, for three or four weeks until it is completed. It is unlikely to need more than ten hours to be spent with the old person in collecting the facts and about another five hours putting it together. It is helpful to write down the agreed details after each session and to read these notes before resuming the conversation. In this way accuracy can be assured, and continuity and genuine interest is demonstrated to the elderly person. The final version, the complete and much prized life history book can be made from the ongoing notes. If the subject has written his or her own record it may need some amendments, but it is almost certainly a mistake to take away the voice of the writer by tidying it up too much or undermining them by over-correcting punctuation and spelling.

It is both interesting and heartening to see how much even confused old people can remember about their lives when gently prompted to do so. Holland and Rabbitt's research (1991) shows that being encouraged to remember increases an aged person's ability to do so. Reminiscence, in groups or in between individuals such as in the preparation of life history books is therefore helpful as well as pleasing. Even gravely withdrawn people seem, given time, gentle and appropriate questions and genuine interest, able to recall past events vividly. Questions such as 'Where did you grow up?', or, 'How did you meet your wife? (or husband?)' rarely fail to elicit lively accounts. In helping to complete a life history book be alert to significant comments that, when recorded, illuminate a relationship or an event. For example Alice who loved the song about the blue gown told in detail of the time and place when she met her John. She told how he was 'right cheeky and followed me all the way home that very first evening whistling "Alice Blue Gown", and do you know he was there when I went out to work the next morning, whistling again. He said he'd been there all night, as if I'd believe that.' Alice giggled like a girl when she talked about this; her listener felt that she knew him. This part of the tape remained Alice's favourite in spite of all of her achievements recorded on the rest of it.

Old people have to give up independent living for many different reasons, including illness in themselves or their partners, or maybe a life crisis of the caring relative or their immediate family. A view widely held is that an old person will be admitted to care because they are alone and no longer able to look after themselves. It is not uncommon however for a husband or wife to have to leave home to go into residential care because their spouse is no longer able to look after them or because children, however concerned, cannot manage to do so. Such a situation is frequently full of not only sadness, but bitterness too, with the frailer partner or very sick parent feeling despair and abandonment and the stronger or younger family member feeling guilt or distress. When one considers the intensity of feeling and the web of experiences that bind people who have shared their lives and grown old together, then separating, however sensible, will always be fraught and painful. Because the feelings are so intense they are frequently not breached for fear that they will be overwhelming. The partings may be handled briskly and insensitively, without discussions and with refuge being taken in the idea that the old person is too frail to face the truth and that it is kinder for them to be allowed to believe that they will return to their own homes 'when they are well' (Gillies, 1992). A life history book prepared either by a third party as a facilitator or by a family member can record in ways that are lasting and containable, the reasons and the feelings about the partings as well as about the quality of the life shared.

Mr and Mrs Bumble illustrate this last point well. Mr Bumble was a heavily-built man in his late seventies who had become confined to a wheelchair. He was impatient with his inefficient old body and irritable and demanding of others. Mrs Bumble was alert, both mentally and intellectually, but she was pounds lighter than her husband. She tired easily and found that she could not cope with the physical and emotional demands of her husband; reluctantly she agreed to his being admitted to residential care. Almost immediately Mr Bumble seemed to deteriorate, he rarely spoke, and when approached by staff and, even more significantly, when visited by his wife, he seemed unable to keep awake. Nevertheless, whether asleep or awake, he looked as if he was bad-tempered. Because of Mr Bumble's moods and Mrs Bumble's distress it was decided to make a life history book working with Mrs Bumble but focusing on Mr Bumble's life. A rich and vivid picture was portrayed by Mrs Bumble; details of a hard childhood, early marriage, of a young couple's struggle to buy the house that they shared together right up to the time when Mr Bumble had to leave were recorded. The book told of Mr Bumble's skill in creating a lovely garden, the apple tree still bearing fruit, and of the pride they shared in their two children. It told how Mrs Bumble favoured the son while Mr Bumble thought the 'moon and stars' shone from his daughter. Recorded too were Mrs Bumble's comments about her husband, who occasionally drank too much, and had a bad temper, but was a hard worker and a good and loving man. Some happy times, including a seaside holiday, were captured. Mrs Bumble went on to record her husband's deteriorating health, her own sense of helplessness when he fell and she was unable to lift him. She told of making her decision to send her husband to a home; she had made this decision alone, believing that her husband was too confused to be party to it, though for the most part, she knew that she could not face his fears and recriminations. Mrs Bumble recorded in the book her sense of sadness and loss about their separation: 'I never go into the garden without thinking of him. He is a lovely man.' When it was finished the book was left with Mr Bumble and a care assistant read this book many times to him. She persisted even when he seemed to be asleep and was rewarded after the third reading not by a word or even a smile but by a hand stretched out showing that he wanted to keep the book. With further readings Mr Bumble no longer pretended to be asleep, he clearly listened intently, commenting occasionally 'it takes you back, doesn't it.' Eventually he was able to weep a little at the ending and gradually he became much less restless and no longer looked so bad-tempered. Eventually both Mr and Mrs Bumble shared the book, Mrs Bumble reading it to him every so often on her visits. It seemed as if focusing on the written word gave their feelings great authority and yet spared some of the intensity of saying those things to each other. The old couple were too tired and weak to discuss matters directly, both had loving things to share as well as regrets but did not have the energy to explore them together. In Mr and Mrs Bumble's case, a third party's role in writing the book seemed essential; she was needed as a bridge between them and as a filter of their overwhelming emotions.

It is sometimes possible for one partner to write the life history book with and for the other. Even so, he or she may need encouragement and support from another person, a family member, friend or social worker, if they are to be able to persist with an honest appraisal of what has happened between them. Life history books, when written by a parent and child or grandchild together, are especially rewarding. Making time in the ordinary routine of a day to talk about a parent's life thus far, and then recording it requires openness and discipline from the child. If the book is approached as a joint venture for other people 'we will write it down for your grandchildren or great-grandchildren to read', this may take some of the embarrassment that people who have lived together for a long time sometimes have in making the unsaid explicit. It can certainly be a vivid proof that the ageing parent has been and still is important to the adult child, and that the continuing family line will be in some way influenced by the old person near the end of their life. For children and grandchildren of those old people from ethnic minorities who have grown up in different places, it is a unique opportunity to learn about their homeland and culture.

It is not too much to expect that at this late stage it is possible still for old problems and wounds to be healed. For example, a middle-aged woman was working with her mother on her life history book. Their relationship had always been turbulent and the daughter was bitter about her mother's reaction to her when she had found herself, in her early twenties, pregnant but still unmarried. Her mother had been punitive, unkind and rejecting and this attitude had persisted for many years; in fact, the breach had never really been mended. In sorting out her mother's papers and preparing some details for the life history book the daughter became aware that her mother had married only after she, too, had been pregnant. The discussion that followed between the mother and daughter was at times angry, hurt and bewildered but the daughter came to understand, if not entirely accept, the displaced guilt that her mother had been showing at the

time as well as her sadness and disappointment that her daughter
had been unable to avoid the same mistakes. Both women, a
generation apart, were in many ways victims of harsh social attitudes towards female sexuality and could acknowledge this and renew
a bond.

The value of bringing to light the sort of secret described here, and
many families have such, is that it allows more open communication
of feelings and facts. Not all discussions between parents and children
have such a dramatic edge but in most parent/child relationships there
exists a tangle of needs, changes and dependencies. Many things that
have not previously been said or said incompletely benefit from
expression particularly at a time when parents and children realise
that time is running out. Poverty and strain in early marriage felt by
the parents may have been sometimes expressed as harshness to the
children. Children may not have understood reasons why parents
separated, or why children were evacuated to the country during the
war, and how these partings felt. Many of the things that have rubbed
sore spots in the relationships can be soothed. For people from
ethnic minorities growing old in a second homeland this time can be
a chance for them to share with their family how they would like to
be treated and respected. Such discussions can be held without a life
history book being prepared, but the book as a focus encourages
communication.

It may not always be possible for someone who has already been
damaged by a serious condition such as Alzheimer's disease to become
involved in a life review simply because their memory is so impaired.
However, it is possible to work on personal reminiscence with a
confused old person and even one already assessed as having
Alzheimer's disease may be able to take part in group reminiscence.
It will take more time and patience to work with someone withdrawn
and confused and it will be necessary to use those periods of time
when the old person seems more in touch with reality. This may mean
taking an opportunistic approach rather than scheduling sessions on
a weekly basis. Time spent quietly with them and personal contact
are in themselves therapeutic, and even if the old person is unable
to read or enjoy the finished book the details and memories recorded
in it will help staff and family carers to relate to him or her as
someone who has achieved much and not just someone who is totally
dependent. Even if one has to collect a history about an old person
from a friend or family, background knowledge can help to plan the
person's care in sensitive and helpful ways, though they may no longer
be able to say what they want for themselves. For example, the
daughter of one very confused old lady told her mother's paid carers
that as a young woman she had had a collection of opera records.
This made it possible to ensure that music she had loved was played

in her room. Afterwards she could be found occasionally singing along with the records; *Tosca* seemed to be her favourite.

Sometimes, when an old person is severely demented, it is only possible to collect details of their long life by working with their children or occasionally their spouse. Helping a family to recapture the occasions that they shared and to tell of their mother's or father's lives when they were young can ease some of the strain and guilt that children may feel at seeing their parents go into residential care or being cared for in the community by strangers. It can provide an opportunity for them to express, to someone outside the family, the strong emotions brought on by witnessing the decline of their parent's health and the inevitability of seeking outside help, and to display, in talking of their gratitude and affection for their parents, their genuine regret. Some parent/child relationships will always produce ambivalent feelings, but sensitive listening can help to highlight the more positive attitudes and to acknowledge duty done well or care carried out meticulously even though the child had mixed feelings for the parent. Preparation of a life history book involving the family of an old person makes a bridge, and enables the children to keep in touch with their parents with ease and even with a sense of pleasure which guilt or anxiety unexpressed could have eroded.

The relationship between a very sick father and his daughter Nadia, was immensely improved after she had been helped to write his life history with him. The old man had come from Cyprus with a young wife and one baby to this country to find work. In their first years here however they suffered acute poverty and lived in very bad conditions. By the time Nadia, the last of five children, was born, the family were much more comfortable but her father never lost his fear of poverty. His daughter said that she remembered him talking only of duty and thrift and never of love or fun. She dreaded having to help to look after him since whenever they met they quarrelled, and he accused her of bringing up her children to be careless and extravagant. It was some time before she could be persuaded to try to get closer to him by finding out more about the reasons for his attitudes. She particularly resented the fact that he had remained mean and controlling to her mother up to her death some years before. Nevertheless she persisted, perhaps because of her father's teaching about duty. Both father and daughter were rewarded and, as she learnt more about his life in Cyprus and about the penury and struggles that he had suffered, she was able to cope with his moods and even tease him out of them. Years of misunderstanding did not go away but enough of their consequences faded away to enable them to make a reasonable reconciliation.

In summary, life reviews are valuable as a means of improving the quality of life of people in their extreme old age, are pleasurable and enhance a sense of self-worth. And they may enable old people towards the end of their lives to reach a philosophical view of their life's experiences and approaching death. If they are recorded in simple, easily accessible ways, then the stories of their lives will intrigue their carers and help to ensure that they are treated as individuals and not just another old and tired person.

HOW TO MAKE A LIFE HISTORY BOOK

Start by explaining to the old person exactly what is suggested and what it might mean to them. Do so in an unthreatening way conveying that it is interest and respect for them that makes it important to write down their life history. Explain that they can keep this record to read or to share with other people if they wish but that it may be read by and be useful to paid carers as well as family and friends.

Set out a timetable, but remember that they may need to be reminded about this quite often. Suggest, for example, meeting for about 40 minutes every Tuesday or Thursday and say 'You can tell me about your life so far, I will write it all down in this big book and each time we meet we will read it together to see what we have said before. When the book is finished you will have it to keep.' If the old person is very confused with only patches of lucidity, use opportunities as they arise and abandon timetabling sessions. Make provision for the book to be kept in a safe place by a staff member rather than by the old person themselves but if doing so be sure to explain to the old person where the book will be kept. Remember that even if they are forgetful they need and deserve this kind of assurance. It is surprising how, even if they seem to have forgotten about the work from one session to the next, they will usually become animated and interested again once they see the book and they will be back in touch with what happened.

Remember that there is no substitute for genuine interest. Ask questions that will reassure the subject of the book and help to keep the flow of memories going. There are obvious questions: Where were you born? What was it like then? Was it a village, was it small, quiet? Did you live in a big house? Who shared the house with you? All these questions will help to bring back memories and give a picture of what their life has been like. Other questions will bring out vivid memories: What was school like for you? What were you good at doing? What lessons did you like best? What didn't you like? What did you do when you left school? Did you want to work there? How much did you earn? What did you do with the money? When did you meet your husband or your wife? What were they like? How long were you courting? When and where did you get married? Where did you live when you were first married? Did you have any children? Where are they now? Do not be too hesitant about asking questions like these though they may seem intrusive. Remember, however, that old people are not used to being valued or listened to, they are often afraid they are boring younger people with their stories. Almost everyone likes to talk to others about how we feel and to share attitudes or events; in doing so, a genuine sense of being close to another person is gained.

The answers to these questions will probably not fill many pages but they will be packed full of interesting ideas. Ask the old person how they would like to see their story recorded, that is, in a scrapbook and handwritten, or typed and more like a conventional book. If the book is to be handwritten use large clear handwriting, writing on one side of the page only. Make sure that the writing is big – remember the old person may not be able to see well. Put in as many photographs as possible, supplementing these with photocopies from a library or other sources. They will be very precious and will certainly attract the attention of any reader or carer who comes along.

Before starting to work with someone old try to have a discussion with another old, but not frail, person. Reflect upon what questions seemed to help the flow of the conversation and how it felt to hear about their reminiscences; ask their advice on preparing life reviews and life history works.

REFERENCES

Butler, R.N. 1963. The Life Review; an interpretation of reminiscences in the Aged. In *Psychiatry*, 26, 368–378.

Coleman, P. 1989. *Ageing and the Reminiscence Process*. John Wiley and Sons, Chichester.

Gillies, C. 1992. The Management of the Move to Dependent Living. Unpublished research, Oxford.

Holland, C.A. and Rabbitt, P.M. 1991. Ageing memory, use versus impairment. In *British Journal of Psychiatry*, 82, 29–38.

Kiernat, J.M. 1979. The use of life review with confused nursing home residents. In *American Journal of Occupational Therapy*, **33**, 306–310.

Norris, A. 1987. *Reminiscence with Elderly People*. Winslow Press, London.

CHAPTER 6

Reminiscence work projects

Reminiscence projects can be as simple or as complex as those involved wish them to be. They may only involve two people, the scribe and the person who is reviewing their life history; or a group of six or eight people meeting in a protected environment such as a purpose-built day centre or hospital. They may involve a group of neighbours or members of a particular ethnic community, or a series of interlinked groups which have come together to make a much larger project. Projects may be as ambitious as some of the reminiscence groups described in this chapter. There are a number of ways of undertaking reminiscence work, all of which are valid provided that they remain true to the principles of reminiscence: that is to provide personal satisfaction, social contact or a chance to complete thinking through life's events. In whatever way it is approached it must feel right to those taking part.

The oral history work that has been done by reminiscence groups shows that the focus of discussion does not always need to be on a person or the group itself; a great deal of valuable work has been done by creating a resource for other people. The resource may be an exhibition or a play, or it could be a book of poetry or a project that uses painting, needlework or crafts.

The examples given here suggest ways in which currently untapped resources in the community could be used to enhance the experience of reminiscence for old people and to produce a book, exhibition or event that has value in its own right. If a group leader uses group-work skills and knowledge of old people to help an artist or writer to work with a group, there can be very exciting results.

The two life history books in this chapter are the stories of real people although, to protect anonymity, their names and some other details have been changed. The three group projects demonstrate co-operative working between professionals and carers and the very old people themselves. The group projects show that it is possible, for groups of old people and for the people who care about them, to produce exhibitions for public show or to shape the script of a professional theatre production. To achieve this, resources that already existed were used; no extra money had to be raised.

EXAMPLES OF LIFE HISTORY BOOKS

Maudie Brown

Background to the Book

Maudie Brown was the oldest inhabitant of a village now largely a dormitory town; she had lived there for well over 60 years. She had no family or friends near her and knew few of the young busy people who were her neighbours. She became increasingly frail and finally fell and broke her hip. She was some time in hospital, eventually moving to a rehabilitation ward where her walking did not improve and it became clear that she would not be able to live alone any longer. It was agreed that she should move into residential care. The ward sister, understanding the enormity of the move for Maudie Brown, suggested to her that it was important that her history and her interesting life so far should be recorded in a life history book that she could take to the residential home with her. The occupational therapist started work with Maudie on the book and they had only spent two sessions together on it when a vacancy came up at the home for Maudie and she moved on. The staff ensured that the knowledge that Maudie had started a life history book was communicated to the home; the home promised that Maudie's key worker would work with her on it, if that was what Maudie wanted. The occupational therapist from the ward promised Maudie that she would visit her in the home once the book was complete, so that Maudie could read it to her.

Maudie's key worker was a young care assistant some 50 years her junior. Working together on the book, they compiled the record that is included here. The project took five weeks to complete, working for about a half-hour a day for about three days each week. It was written in large bold handwriting on A3 size paper. Pictures from Maudie's own collection were pasted in it alongside the writing. This particular life history book is included here because, although it is not long, it captures some of the spirited personality of Maudie both as a young woman and as an old frail one. It is written in the first person as Maudie has such an engaging way of expressing herself.

Some details have been changed to respect confidentiality.

The outside of the book bears the legend 'Some details of Maudie Brown's life written down by Joan Cross – care assistant, Cannons Lodge, May 1989'.

I was born in Hull in 1910 and I was christened Maud Anastasia Mabel, would you believe it. My mother always had high flying ideas but I don't know why because we were as poor as church mice and as common as muck. My dad was a labourer, a hod carrier on the buildings. He was often out of work and he was never the same after he came back from the war so he didn't work very much. My mum used to help out with money by working as a kitchen hand in the local bakery. She often used to work very hard and had to leave us alone at night. Who was us? Well there were eight kids in all: I had five brothers and two sisters, I was in the middle. We all got on quite well but I remember that I loved my oldest brother the best. At night, when my mum was out, we all used to share two beds in one room, top to tail, and my brother used to keep us all quiet telling us stories, he had a gift for it. Sometimes he used to tell us ghost stories and we would all squeal and hide under the bed clothes.

I didn't like school, you see I wasn't clever. We were often late because my mum was too tired to get us up in the mornings and I used to get caned for being late and I used to think that wasn't fair. I guess I was a bit cheeky too so maybe I deserved some of the tellings off. Anyway, when I left school I was 12 or so, I could hardly read properly but I was good at sums. I looked quite smart too. I had lovely long red hair and I was very vain about it. I used to put it in rags at night to make it curl, it used to hurt to sleep on them but I reckoned it was worth it.

I was sent into service when I was 13. That was very, very hard. The thing I remember most about those years was having really sore chapped hands; my hands were always red and sometimes bled because they were so dry from being in cold water and using all the harsh polishes. In those days you know we used to use soda for washing and that really was hard on the hands. All my life I've wanted to have nothing much more than long red fingernails like they have in the movies.

I met Joe, my husband when I was 17, we were married six years later. In those days you had to court for a long time because we didn't have any money you see. He was the only sweetheart I ever had, although I made eyes at few others I can tell you. Yes, I was a flirt but I really only wanted Joe. We moved into our little cottage that belonged to Mr Harrow the farmer, when we were married. I thought it was absolute heaven. I made all the curtains and I made the rugs for the floor from rags. We got a sofa and a chair from my employer;

they weren't much good, they were second, if not third hand, but then she always was a miserable old thing. We saved up for the bed. I fell pregnant early on but we lost the baby. Just think he would have been nearly 60 had he lived. I still wonder what he would have looked like. Joe was a tall good-looker, would he have been like him his dad I ask. We never had no more children. The doctor said to me only a few years ago that something, I can't remember the long words, went wrong in my womb when I had my boy and if it had happened nowadays they could have put it right easily and I could have had any number of kids. Joe and I were very sad not to have any of our own. We went on trying, I don't say we didn't enjoy trying but having a baby of your own must be quite something special. I looked after most of my nephews and nieces from time to time but it didn't quite make up for it. Anyway not having kids meant we weren't very short of money. Joe stayed working at the farm even after it was sold and another man took over. He never went away to the war because he didn't have a good chest and anyway it was thought that farm work was some kind of special contribution to the country. I had to help on the farm too at that time and it was hard, do you know I really enjoyed it in spite of the fact that I had lived in a town all my childhood. I started to breed my dogs about this time, I got into it by chance really. The farmer's wife was a silly towny woman and she couldn't cope when her bitch was having the pups and so I went along to help. They were Border Collies. I had a pup from her and then the next year I had another one and I started to breed from them and I was best at Crufts two years running with them. Now that's something isn't it, there was me, no education, nothing much really to my name, and yet I did really well and beat a whole lot of other people to it. I was right proud.

Joe got really ill when he was about 50 and I had to nurse him day and night. I did my duty, but there were times when I could have run off I'll tell you. Imagine having to wipe a grown man's bottom and care for him like a baby. I didn't ask for any help from anybody, however I am sure Joe was pleased I kept him at home. I remember some good things about that time though; I remember sitting by his bed in the dark when we listened to the wireless together. We loved plays on it. I never think television is as good. We had some cosy time together just then and when he went I was very lonely. Life has never felt the same again. But I continued with my dogs, in fact, I had them right up to about five years ago. And I'll tell you I've had another proposal of marriage, yes I wasn't past it. He lived in the next village but I thought he was looking for someone to look after him and I wasn't that daft, I'd had enough of that.

I quite like living in this place now though I thought I'd never stop crying when I had to leave the cottage, it was all the memories you see.

The garden especially. But here there are people to talk to and it is quite nice having someone to look after me for a change. I know I shan't last a lot longer, well let's face it, 84 years is enough for anyone. What am I proud of? Well, yes, I am proud of some things, I never owed anybody a penny in my life and I have even paid for my funeral now. I was a good wife though I nagged a bit I expect, and I taught myself to read proper, well, I mean I had to if I was going to work with dogs. I have got a lot of nice memories dear, thank you for asking.

Errol May

Background to the book

This is the life history of an elderly black man, Errol May, prepared when he agreed to attend a day-care centre five days a week.

Mr May had been a widower for ten years. His health had deteriorated steadily after his wife's death and his one child, a son, lived and worked a hundred miles away. The father and son relationship had never been good but the son had started to become closer to his father when he became involved in arranging for his father's day care. The son was very critical of the day-care centre and considered that the staff had given insufficient thought to integrating a black man into a centre staffed entirely by white people and where all the others attending were white.

The manager of the centre suggested that if Mr May prepared a life history book when he started attending the centre he could use this to reaffirm his own identity in a strange place. Also, if he wanted to, he could share it with the care staff and others who attended the centre to help them to understand him and some of the difficulties and differences old people experience when growing old in a second homeland. In addition, it could also be something that Mr May could share with his grandchildren.

Mr May's son liked this suggestion and began to feel that there was a real concern for his father's welfare by the centre's manager.

The centre had as well as paid staff, two voluntary helpers who came in twice a week to help organise social activities; both volunteers were retired women. After meeting one of the volunteers, both Mr May and his son agreed that working with this volunteer on a life history book was a good idea and the son took time off work to help his father and the volunteer. Father and son between them were able to find a few family photographs and some postcards of Jamaica to illustrate the book. Mr May fitted well into the centre and said how much he had enjoyed making his life history book and how much it had meant to him. Others attending the centre were curious about it and it became a common sight to see Mr May sitting with another of the centre's attenders reading to them from details of his life history. The success of the project also led the centre's manager to decide to help make a life history book for each of those attending the centre who would like one.

Mr May's life history book is written rather formally in the third person. This style echoed the reserve of both father and son. It has also been altered slightly to respect confidentiality.

Errol May's life history

Mr Errol May was born in Kingston in Jamaica in 1919. He was named after his grandfather and his father. There has always been a man named Errol in the May family. Mr May was the eldest son. He remembers lots of loving, lots of noise and bustle in house and yard where family and friends seem to be always coming and going. He says that he was happy always as a child, that he can remember being scolded for not doing what he was told, but he can remember being hugged more often.

He started at St. Mary's School when he was seven and was caned once for being late; he was never late again! He learned about the British Empire at school, the map was red where the country was British, Jamaica was red.

On Sunday evenings the whole family would gather, with grand-mother at the centre, and sing hymns together.

Mr May worked in an engineering factory in the Southern US during the Second World War. Black men could not speak to white women and had to get off the side walk if someone white came along.

When the US would not give any more work permits and there was no work back home he thought he would go to Britain – the 'Mother Country' – she was offering work and a loan to cover the cost of the journey. He was sad to leave his home, his family and especially to leave his girlfriend Merial, but he believed that he could come back home in a few years once he had made good money. When he arrived at Tilbury docks it was raining and so cold.

A friend had given him an address where he could stay until he found somewhere. He quickly found work in a car factory. Pay was good if you were prepared to do overtime and Mr May was a hard worker so he made good wages. That was when he lived in a hostel with other West Indian men. Although the men tended to stick together Mr May made many friends from white people. He was chosen to play in the pub darts team at that time and travel around with them. People were curious about him as a black man; one woman asked if she could touch his skin and was surprised that it was quite soft!

He made a good friend then, a white man, who worked next to him on the production line and who stayed a friend right up to his death two years ago. This man, Frank Edwards, and the church were Mr May's best support during the time that Mrs May was ill with cancer and when she died.

When Mr May felt ready to settle down and make a family of his own, he sent for Merial but learned that she was courting another man and that she didn't want to leave Jamaica. Mr May married Anna two years after that. Anna was also from Jamaica and had come to join her parents in Britain when she was sixteen, three years earlier. They were married on 16 April, Anna's twentieth birthday. Anna was as good a wife as he could ever have hoped for and when she died ten years ago a light went out. Errol and Anna had one son, Errol. Errol is clever. He went to college and got a degree in Engineering. Errol now has two children of his own.

The two Errols, father and son, did not always get on. The son is angry at the racism and oppression of black people in Britain. The older Errol thinks things are better in Britain nowadays and that even when he first came to Britain he usually felt welcome and work had been easy to find, when there had been no work back home, and being polite costs nothing.

Soon after he and Anna moved into the council house where he still lives, people said that he ought to go back home and leave the house for a white family.

He is not going to leave the house yet; he goes to the centre on weekdays and to church when he can on Sundays. Mr May is proud of his fifty years' membership of the Car Workers Club and of his exemplary employment record. He is proud too of the help that he has been able to give through his church.

Mr May wishes that there were more people around now to talk to about what life was like in Jamaica but above all he wishes that Anna was still around. He is proud of his son and he hopes that Errol and his wife Lorraine and his grandchildren Errol junior, Linette and Judy will enjoy his short book about his life.

REMINISCENCE BY A LOCAL COMMUNITY

In conjunction with a community education worker, a clergyman used reminiscence to create a community feeling amongst older people on a housing estate that lacked a sense of community. Together they documented the history of the area and created an exhibition for the local library.

The clergyman, from a team working from an inner-city church, had been given responsibility for a daughter church on the housing estate and encouraged to do outreach work. He undertook a community audit and found that in the older style council housing surrounding this tiny church, a very high proportion of the people living there were now elderly, having first moved into the houses when they were built in the 1920s or soon afterwards. There was no community focus, no specific services for elderly people in that area and a number of the elderly people that he talked to were frightened of going out because of a perceived threat of attack from younger people. He wanted, therefore, to establish a project that was local and would focus on elderly people who were socially isolated and comparatively poor. Such a project would give him, as a Christian and a clergyman, an opportunity to serve the community without becoming 'heavy' about religion.

He established contact with a community education worker who was funded for a half-day weekly to work with elderly people in a community that included the clergyman's patch. After approaching a few people on the estate he established that there were six elderly people who would like to come together and take part in a reminiscence project.

One of the elderly men who said he would be interested in taking part in the project offered his house as a meeting place. The community education worker tape-recorded much of the discussion in the early meetings and produced transcripts for the following meeting. The meetings started in a slightly tentative manner. However, the man who had offered to act as host started to write down his thoughts and memories and some of the discussions that had occurred, something that he had not done since he had left school. He then took over from the community education worker as group scribe.

The group decided to focus on the area and to talk about how the housing estate came to be what it was and their own memories and past experiences of living there. The group grew quickly more confident, and it became clear early on that they wanted to do more with the material that they were producing than simply share it with each other. The community education worker approached the local librarian who was very interested in holding an exhibition and was able to find for the group photographs of the estate fifty years before. The librarian even found photographs of the site prior to the building of the estate from the library's local studies section. The text and the comments on the photographs were supplied by the group members who took considerable pride, quite appropriately, in the exhibition that they had created. They recorded details about the area and made a unique contribution to the history of the city and its people.

The marriage of the man who hosted the group to his neighbour whom he had not spoken to prior to the group was an added bonus for everyone and naturally took place in the local church!

REMINISCENCE WORK AND A MUSEUM EXHIBITION

A group of women from an Afro-Caribbean community which had been established for thirty years were keen to record the memories and experiences of their older members. Several of the older members were returning to the Caribbean for good and some had already died. The women feared that the memories of how the community had been created and developed would be lost, and the younger generation would not know about how they and their community came to be living in this part of Britain. Even before it was completed the project had done much to bring together older and younger generations and to help young people understand what the experience was like of leaving home and country and making a new life in a new and not always welcoming land.

The women who wanted to make recordings of their elders took the initiative and contacted the Museum Service, on the suggestion of a community worker. The Museum Service and the women agreed that the Museum Service would fund a project that would work towards an exhibition at the local museum about the Afro-Caribbean community in the 1950s and 60s and their lives and work in the town. As a result of the project the museum has been able to add oral history tape recordings and some donated objects to its collection. The collection of tape recordings was made over a period of about four months by the women, and the older people offered photographs and objects that they had brought with them from the West Indies.

Initially, the project had some hiccoughs as none of those taking part had previous experience of working in this way. However, the museum education officer, a white woman, was able to support them though, in line with the group's wishes, she did not carry out any of the interviews or take part in the reminiscence groups. She supplied the women with a tape recorder and arranged a day of training on how to use the equipment and how to structure interviews. This day did much to bring the organisers together and helped them to focus upon what they were recording and what to do with the information afterwards.

The local West Indian Day Centre became the centre of the project, as there people had the time to sit, talk and encourage each other in recalling events in their lives. It was also a friendly place for the volunteers to visit and make their tape recordings. The first reminiscence sessions were used to establish who would make the recordings and what would be committed onto tape. These sessions proved so enjoyable that they continued after the project and the exhibition were over! People wanting to know how to start projects using reminiscence would visit the centre to seek advice.

There was a tremendous sense of satisfaction and pride as people realised that their own hardships and contribution to the life of the town were being recognised by a public exhibition. The exhibition attracted both public interest and the offer of a funded arts worker to run a series of writing workshops at the centre.

REMINISCENCE WORK AND A PROFESSIONAL THEATRE PRODUCTION

In 1989, to commemorate the outbreak of the Second World War 50 years earlier, a network of museums throughout the country were creating exhibitions. The BBC and Independent Television both gave the outbreak of war considerable coverage. At the same time the local museum service decided to incorporate its contribution to commemorating 1939 into a wider approach which could be used in subsequent exhibitions about other subjects. They decided to focus on change, which included both immigration and emigration from the area, and how world and other events changed people's lives. Their 1939 exhibition was to be called 'Memories of Change'.

The local professional touring theatre company received funding from the local council on a number of conditions, one of which was that it produced plays that drew on local issues and were locally relevant. At the same time, a community worker employed by Social Services was trying to establish reminiscence work as a valid activity in hospitals, residential and day-care settings. As she was already involved with the museum service, and knew the theatre company's conditions of funding, she approached the residential and day care establishments to see if they would be interested in using a writer to create a script for a play, using people's memories of 1939, that would complement the museum's 'Memories of Change' exhibition. They were. The community worker then introduced the writer to two residential homes for elderly people, and two day-care centres, that already had successful reminiscence groups. People in the four locations were invited to join special reminiscence groups that would understand the writer's brief and work with her in order to help her to write the script for the play, which was called 'Last Bus to Wanstock'.

The play focused on Freda, an elderly lady who now lived in a residential home but who left the home for one day, in order to take the bus to Wanstock where she had grown up and had lived her adult life. As the play took us through the day she reflected upon her girlhood and young adult life up to the outbreak of war. Both project and play were successes. In addition to performances in the participating homes, the play toured the area.

For the care staff, both those who had been involved in the partici-pating groups and those who had not, there was considerable pride in the contribution their home or centre had made to the play. However it is fair to say that the knowledge that their groups and their memories had contributed to this professional production was lost on a number of the more frail and confused group members.

It should also be said that talking about the Second World War produced some painful memories for group members. The groups stuck bravely to their agreed task of providing material for the author. Supported by the community worker, the staff involved in the project made sure that all those who had taken part had time to discuss the painful aspects of 1939 and the war, either one-to-one, or, if they preferred, in a group.

SUMMARY

This chapter has given five examples of reminiscence work, under-taken by a variety of paid and voluntary workers in a variety of settings. The examples given illustrate a range of ways of working, some more ambitious than others.

Before embarking on a reminiscence project, it is vital to spend time thinking both about what approach would most benefit the old people concerned, and about who is available to become involved in the project. The guidelines for planning and running a group, given in Chapter 4, will help with this.

CHAPTER 7

Building a resource bank

This book advocates an approach to work with old people that respects and uses their memories to ease communication with them, to create opportunities for pleasure and enjoyment shared with others, and to facilitate reflections on their long lives. There are many different ways of achieving these goals; only some of them are discussed here but all need to be resourced, sometimes with knowledge, concern and time from others, and sometimes with a range of practical tools. This chapter describes how to create a bank of resources that will help work both with small groups and with individuals; and to start to undertake projects on a larger scale.

ESTABLISHING RESOURCE NETWORKS

In life history work, reminiscence work and in larger-scale projects, established models or methods of working with younger people have to be adapted for work with older people. Each old person is unique and their diverse networks may be rather damaged, largely because they have lived for a long time, and also, perhaps, because of experiences earlier in their lives. In order to sustain work with old people, the boundaries that surround the organisations and institutions on which our society is based must be removed to help to create a network and resource bank to facilitate the work. This is neither an easy process nor a rapid one: networks and resource banks need continual servicing in order to ensure that they can deliver what is needed in order to make the right things happen.

The world of very old people is bounded by organisations and institutions that provide services to them. Each of the organisations is very clear about what it can provide and where its boundaries are but old people can be locked into receiving a service in a way that isolates them and leaves them feeling helpless and dependent. For example, a volunteer who delivers meals on wheels to an old woman sees that she is desperately lonely and longing for someone to talk to. The volunteer may not have time to talk and may not know what services exist to help the old lady, so she simply continues to deliver meals and cuts her short when she attempts to start a conversation. In another situation a district nurse calling twice-weekly to dress an old man's leg ulcers could never stay to hear the end of his stories, but if she had known that the local school was doing a history project and looking for old people to help with it, she could have suggested that the old man might have liked to become involved. Another example is of a museum education worker who may be charged with developing a service for older people but who may not know any older people or where to start – she may work hard but still produce an inappropriate exhibition. In all these instances the good intentions of concerned people are limited by the boundaries of the services, and old people may be isolated as a result. Resourcing reminiscence work will mean cutting across these boundaries. This can pose an interesting challenge to a worker, who has to try and create a network of contacts of people and resources that will help current projects and also create opportunities for people both to give to and gain from reminiscence.

When creating a network of resources it is useful to keep a comprehensive written list of who people are, where they are and why they want to be involved. This list should be regularly reviewed to ensure that it is kept current. A resource bank for reminiscence work is not like a deposit account in a bank or building society; its resources cannot be tucked away and called upon when needed. It needs active servicing, and ways of adding to and updating the bank need to be devised. In addition to 'depositing' information on local people and resources in a resource bank, workers should find out how specialist organisations can help. Some of these may have local branches; others may be able to help from a distance by sending literature and advice. Though networks and resource banks take time to build up, there are a great many readily accessible resources, and it is often just a question of knowing where to look, who to ask, a little lateral thinking, persuasion and persistence. In creating a resource bank, as in other areas of work, the aspects that are most likely to last are those that provide mutual benefit, in this case to the resource and the project. Providing feedback to those who are resourcing projects is extremely important. This can be done in a number of ways: by inviting them to an event, by providing photographs or by verbal and written reports.

A good way to start collecting information for a resource bank is by preparing and circulating a press release. This should explain what reminiscence work is, describe the particular project or projects, who is involved and what the project needs in the way of resources whether objects, volunteers, photographs or music. A contact name, address and telephone number should be included in the press release and the times when the contact will be available. This can be sent to local radio and newspapers, the editors of newsletters or circulars of the organisations being targeted, and to individuals who are felt to be potential sources of help. When creating a network of resources, do not overlook the old people themselves and all that they have to contribute. People who have their age in common will not necessarily also share common backgrounds or interests so, in addition to providing the project with resources, they can help focus the work and by implication the resources needed for it. They can often provide much more than workers expect, either through their personal mementos and photographs collected over many years, or through recollections and details of their lives.

In organisations or institutions, the best starting point is a member of staff who is sympathetic to reminiscence work and who is prepared to defend it and argue its benefits and to advise on how best to publicise the project. They may be prepared to do this for one of a number of reasons; because they have a relative who is old, or they have tried this kind of work themselves and have been thwarted, or even because they have a small amount of money that they want to spend on enhancing the quality of their patients' or clients' lives and are unsure where to start. Almost all residential or nursing homes, day centres and hospitals want to provide satisfying social or recreational activities for the people that they are looking after. Many employ staff – nurses, care staff, volunteers, occupational therapists or art workers – whose task it is to provide these activities. By working in partnership a project will stand to gain a great deal and the likelihood of reminiscence work flourishing is increased by having a member of staff committed to the project. However, it will take time.

It is important to find out how specialist organisations can help. Some of these, such as Age Concern, will have local branches and others may be able to help from a distance by sending literature, help and advice. The list below gives details of some national and local organisations.

Books, both fiction and non-fiction, are a valuable resource. Short stories, poems, plays and novels can be very powerful in taking readers into the world of old people and so helping them to understand some of the preoccupations of old age, by portraying and explaining other cultures, other places and other times. Television programmes, films and videos that focus on the past, current affairs, life in different parts of the world, or on local communities can also be useful sources of material.

The remainder of this chapter supplies some basic building blocks from which workers can develop their own resource banks. These building blocks include television, film, video, books, fiction and non-fiction, organisations, museums and archives.

ORGANISATIONS AND NETWORKS

National

Age Concern England, 1268 London Road, London SW16 4ER. Tel: 081 679 8000

Age Concern Northern Ireland, 3 Lower Crescent, Belfast BT7 1NR. Tel: 0232 245729.

Age Concern Scotland, 54A Fountainbridge, Edinburgh EH3 9PT. Tel: 031 228 5656.

Age Concern Wales, 4th floor, 1 Cathedral Rd, Cardiff CF1 9SD. Tel: 0222-37156. Age Concern is a confederation of over 1000 national and local organisations concerned with the well-being and happiness of old people. At a national level it provides assistance, advice and specific grants through its network of field officers. It produces a catalogue of its own publications.

Age Exchange, 11 Blackheath Village, London SE3 9LA Tel: 081 318 9105. Has both a theatre company and a museum in South London. They also run workshops and projects and a reminiscence-box loan scheme, and publish pamphlets and booklets about reminiscence.

BASE [British Association for Services to the Elderly], 119 Hassell Street, Newcastle under Lyme, Staffs ST5 1AX. Runs courses, day workshops on work with elderly people. These include courses on reminiscence work.

Help the Aged, St James's Walk, London EC1R 0BE. Publishes a quarterly magazine, *Reminiscence*.

The Imperial War Museum, Lambeth Rd, London SE1 6HZ. Tel: 071 416 5000. Covers all aspects of the First and Second World Wars as well as other conflicts involving Britain and the Commonwealth since 1914.

Manchester Reminiscence Project, Ladywell Hospital, Salford M5 2AA. Provides both written material and workshops.

The National Sound Archive, 29 Exhibition Road, London SW7 2AS. Has a collection of recordings and voices famous and not-so-famous, giving speeches or recalling historic events.

Nostalgia Unlimited, Rainhill, Prescot, Merseyside L35 0QH. Sells reminscence aids.

The Shape Network The umbrella name for a nationwide network of companies that creates opportunities in the arts for people who are disabled or disadvantaged. The local council's arts officer will advise if there is a local Shape company and on their areas of work.

University of the Third Age Brings together older people to study and develop new interests. The local library should have information on local branches.

English Tourist Board, Thames Tower, Blacks Rd, Hammersmith, London W6 9EL. Tel: 081 846 9000.

Northern Irish Tourist Board, St Anne's Court, 59 North St, Belfast BT1 1NB. Tel: 0232 246609.

Scottish Tourist Board, 23 Ravelston Terrace, Edinburgh EH4 3EV. Tel: 031 332 2433.

Welsh Tourist Board, Brunel House, 2 Fitzalan Rd, Cardiff CF2 1UY. Tel: 0222 499 909. Tourist Boards can advise of places of historic interest and give the address of the local tourist board.

Winston Churchill's Britain at War Theme Museum, 64–66 Tooley St, London SE1 2TF. Tel: 071 403 3171. Recreates the life for ordinary British people during the Second World War, including the blackout, Anderson shelters and rationing.

HMS *Belfast*, Morgan's Lane, London SE1. HMS *Belfast* saw action in the Second World War and is now open as a museum which gives a very direct insight into what life at sea in wartime was like.

The Royal British Legion Pilgrimage Department, Royal British Legion Village, Aylesford, Kent ME13 7NX. Tel: 0622 716729/716182. Organises tours and trips to historic sites such as battlefields.

Local

Age Concern is more than likely to have a local branch; the address and telephone number will be in the telephone directory. It will be able to provide information it has received from the national office of Age Concern and information on what exists locally. Many Age Concerns run day centres, befriending services and transport schemes. They may well be able to help with establishing reminiscence work, or indeed already be running groups.

Local museum services – Often there is a curator or an education officer responsible for working with the community who will use local or social history to do this. Some museums lend objects for use in reminiscence work and have created special packs or boxes for this purpose. If they cannot lend objects themselves they may know of other sources locally for obtaining objects. They may also be able to help with old photographs, photocopies of old newspapers or other printed materials.

Local museums and places of historic interest – The local branch of the Tourist Board will have information on these. They should be listed in the local telephone directory or contact one of the main tourist boards for their address.

Local studies – Many libraries or universities have collections of local photographs or film covering the last century. For example the East Anglian Film Archive at the University of East Anglia has produced a video *Norwich 1909–1939* from a selection of films in their archive. The Centre for Oxfordshire Studies at Oxford's Central Library has a collection of photographs of streets and roads in the area and the people who lived in them, that spans the last hundred years. They will provide photocopies of these photographs.

The library service – Libraries buy books and resources both on professional advice and advice from local people and may well be prepared to buy books, pamphlets, audio- and videotapes relevant to reminiscence as part of their general collection. Libraries also have collections of large print books.

Local newspapers – The local newspaper office will have copies on microfiche or in store and may be prepared to issue photocopies of these. Newspaper headlines, articles or advertisements can all be excellent triggers for reminiscence discussion or used to illustrate reminiscence work life history books.

Local history groups or societies – These are usually a very good source of information. If they include someone who is keen on recent history they could help greatly with local sources of objects to borrow and people to talk to.

Students – Many nurses, social workers, psychologists, teachers and clergy will be spending part of their course on placement. Course tutors may be able and willing to encourage students to take part in reminiscence work whilst on placement. Using a student to work in reminiscence or write a life history book with an old person will not cost managers anything, thus they are a very useful and cost-effective resource.

Schools – Using real memories is an important part of recording history and many schools are keen for their pupils to talk or write to old people about their memories as part of the history or humanities curriculum.

The Community Education Service is part of the local education authority and is committed to providing educational opportunities in their widest sense to adults. Workers there may well be interested in co-operating on a reminiscence project or event.

The Workers Education Association (WEA) offers a similar service in many areas.

Local junk shops or car boot sales – Household and other objects can often be bought for small amounts.

Churches or religious groups may wish to undertake reminiscence work or life history books with old people.

BOOKS AND VISUAL AIDS

It is difficult to understand how it feels to be old and dependent. Included here are some books that give vivid, sometimes moving and sometimes challenging, views of old age. The list is not extensive, but it acknowledges the value of both academic and practical texts and creative literature to the development of empathy. Readers will want to add to it from their own reading.

Working with old people

People in society

Deacon, J. 1974 *Joey.* **The National Society for Mentally Handicapped Children and Adults** and **Scribner's.** The autobiography of Joey Deacon, born in 1920, who spent his life in a hospital for physically and mentally handicapped peple. Joey was permanently in a wheelchair with unintelligible speech, unintelligible, that is, until the 1960s when he met Ernie, another inmate who could understand him. Ernie listened to Joey's story, repeated it to Michael who wrote it down, and Tom, who could not read, typed it letter-by-letter at the rate of four or five lines a day.

Goffman, E. 1960. *Asylums: Essays on the Social Situation of Mental Patients and Others.* **Penguin.** Goffman describes the effect that institutions have on both staff and inmates, how institutions develop their own models of normal behaviour and the powerlessness of the individual inmate.

Gray, M., and MacKenzie, H. 1982. *Caring For Older People.* **Penguin.** An easy-to-read book that describes how growing old affects us physically and mentally. It contains a practical guide to caring for older people.

Stevenson, Olive. 1989. *Age and Vulnerability.* **Edward Arnold** for **Age Concern.** This is a wise book containing much useful information and is easy to read because of the author's style and evident concern for older people. It will also add to one's understanding of different cultures.

Victor, C.R. 1987. *Old Age in Modern Society.* **Chapman and Hall.** The book addresses the two aspects of the social dimensions of ageing: the individual's experience, which changes as life takes its course, and the much less flexible socially defined experience.

Mental and physical health

Christie, Agatha. 1971. *By the Pricking of My Thumbs.* **Fontana.** A sensitive view of confusion in old age.

Clarke, Elizabeth. 1965. *The Darkening Green.* **White Lion.** She describes the onset of her husband's blindness by describing the changing seasons of the year, as seen by him for the last time.

Dickens, Monica. 1966. *The Room Upstairs.* **Heinemann.** Eighty-year-old Sybil loses her independence after breaking her leg. Lucid moments are mixed with her confusion and hallucinations; she knows she is declining and fears that she may be admitted to residential care.

Jack, Michael. 1981. *Life Among the Dead.* **Cortney Publications.** A churchyard maintenance man and gardener who has partial hearing, describes the limitations and loneliness of being deaf and puts forward his philosophy of life.

Newton, Ellen. 1980. *This Bed My Centre.* **Virago.** A moving picture of dependency is drawn using the diary that Ellen Newton kept as she was a resident or a patient in a number of homes and hospitals.

Wattis, J. 1993. *Practical Psychiatry in Old Age.* **Chapman and Hall.** This practical manual provides comprehensive information on conditions, their treatment and management. It also emphasises the importance of multi-disciplinary work and of treating the whole person rather than just the condition.

Woolf, Virgina. 1975. *Mrs Dalloway.* **Sussex University Press.** This novel is based on Virginia Woolf's own experience of madness: she had a breakdown in 1904.

Wright, H.T. 1975. *The Matthew Tree.* **Pantheon Books.** A daughter describes her father's last seven years of life, as finally, after a series of strokes, he faces death.

Grief and death

De Beauvoir, Simone. 1969. *A Very Easy Death.* **Penguin.** A moving account of the impact of her mother's death on the author.

Green, J.B., and Green, M.A. 1991. *Dealing with Death.* **Chapman and Hall.** This comprehensive work of reference also includes an excellent section on religious, ethnic and cultural aspects of dying.

Gunzberg, J. 1993. *Unresolved Grief.* **Chapman and Hall.** He considers what causes unresolved grief and what its manifestations are. The book includes case studies and creative exercises.

Hunter, Molly. 1975. *A Sound of Chariots.* **Collins.** Bridie adored her father: she is coming to terms with his death but is unable to cope with her mother's pain. Set at the end of the First World War.

Kübler-Ross, E. 1973. *On Death and Dying.* **Tavistock, London.** A readable and important work on grieving.

Lewis, C.S. 1961. *A Grief Observed.* **Faber and Faber.** A Christian honestly charts the progress of his grief after his wife's death.

Pincus, Lily. 1974. *Death and the Family.* **Faber and Faber.** A wise and warm book about coping with grief, enriched by the author's personal experiences on the death of her husband.

Simenon, Georges. 1968. *The Patient.* **Penguin.** This is a powerful novel about a high-achieving man who is suddenly struck down with a stroke.

Ways of working

Bornat, J. ed. 1994. *Reminiscence Reviewed: Perspectives, Evaluations, Achievements.* **Open University Press.** Written by academics and practitioners, this book reinforces the value of reminiscence and provides a useful overview of research and life review, with particular reference to work with less able people.

Finlay, L. 1993. *Group Work in Occupational Therapy.* **Chapman and Hall.** Explores the practice of group work particularly in psychosocial settings.

Heap, K. 1977. *Group Theory for Social Workers.* **Pergamon.** A well-researched book that examines groups and groupwork in a wide variety of settings.

Karris, B. and Abbod, N. 1985. *Down Memory Lane: Topics and Ideas for Reminiscence Groups.* **Eldersong Publications Inc. USA.**

Tuft, Nancy. 1993. *Arranging Outings for Older People.* **Age Concern. Winslow Press, 9 London Lane, London E8 3PR.** Produce reminiscence packs, which include photographs, tape recordings and other materials, such as *The Reminiscence Quiz Book* by Mike Sherman (1991).

Lives of old people

Cairns, Elizabeth, ed. 1993. *Singing in Tune with Time: Stories and Poems about Ageing.* **ACE Books, co-published by Virago and Age Concern.** Writings by women ranging in mood from Penelope Lively's look at a party where the oldest and the youngest members of the family behave best and enjoy it most, to stories of unwanted old people and one of a quite fearsome granny.

Dhondy, Farrukh. 1986. *Come to Mecca.* **Fontana.** A book of enchanting short stories about black and Asian children growing up in Britain. They give an insight into the lives of youngsters from impoverished families that may help to understand the feelings and attitudes of some black and Asian people who have grown old here.

Hanley, James 1973. *A Woman in the Sky.* **Deutsch.** Two old women living in a high-rise block depend on each other, and both drink. When one is arrested for shoplifting the other jumps from her window and is killed. The vulnerability of the two women is portrayed well as are the social causes of their circumstances.

Schweitzer, Pam, ed. 1984. *A Place to Stay: Memories of Pensioners from Many Lands.* **Age Exchange Theatre Company.** A series of short biographies by old people from different parts of the world who are growing old in Britain.

Spark, Muriel. 1959. *Memento Mori.* **Penguin.** Miss Taylor, the companion of a famous writer, is forced by her crippling arthritis to move to live on a geriatric ward.

Spokes Symonds, Ann. 1989. *Celebrating Age: An Anthology.* **Age Concern.** A collection of quotations that embody the idea that age is a time of growth and a time to celebrate.

Europe and Britain

Lee, Laurie. 1970. *Cider With Rosie.* **Penguin.** Laurie Lee writes about his experience of growing up as the only boy with his mother and his older sisters in an English village early this century.

Thompson, Flora. 1954. *Lark Rise to Candleford.* Describes the life she and her family led in an English hamlet in the early part of the century. Village characters, their jobs and their foibles are all beautifully described. The book has been dramatised and might make an enjoyable theatre outing for you or your group.

Hattersley, Roy. 1983. *A Yorkshire Boyhood.* **Oxford.** An only child growing up in the 1930s in Sheffield and living through the Blitz, winning his 11 plus to grammar school and gaining a place at university.

Any novels by Mary Wesley published by Black Swan. In particular:

The Camomile Lawn. **1985.** Five young cousins gather at their aunt's house in Cornwall for their annual ritual of a holiday, in August 1939. The book tells their story and that of their family and friends over the next 45 years.

A Sensible Life. **1990.** Flora, aged ten, holidays with her parents in Britanny in 1926, as many middle-class English families did. Mary Wesley draws absorbing pictures of what life was like as she tells Flora's story over the next forty years.

War

Briggs, Susan. 1975. *Keep Smiling Through: The Home Front 1939 – 1945.* **Weidenfeld and Nicolson.**

Gershon, Karen, ed. 1989. *We Came as Children.* **Papermac.** A collective biography of 234 Jewish authors all of whom were refugees.

Lewis, Peter 1986. *A People's War.* **A Channel Four Book, Thames Methuen.**

MacDonald, Lyn. 1993. *1915: The Death of Innocence.* **Headline.** The ordinary dogged heroism of the men in the First World War told in their own words.

Miller, Russell. 1993. *Nothing Less Than Victory: The Oral History of D-Day.* **Michael Joseph.** A vivid and intimate account of what it was like to be part of D-Day drawn from letters, diaries, official reports and the oral testimony of veterans.

Black Africa

Lamb, D. 1984. *The Africans.* **Vintage.** This book examines the state of African nations in the late twentieth century in the light of their histories, both tribal and colonial.

The Caribbean

Kogorzinski, Jan. 1992. *A Brief History of the Caribbean: From the Arawak and the Carib to the Present.* **Facts on File, New York and Oxford.**

Naipaul, V.S. 1961. *A House for Mr Biswas.* **Penguin.** This and other of V.S. Naipaul's early books tell the stories of ordinary people living in Trinidad in the early twentieth century. Life was hard, the landscape baked by the sun, and people created the best living they could.

China and Hong Kong

Morris, Jan. 1988. *Hong Kong: Epilogue to an Empire.* **Penguin.**

Mo, Timothy. 1982. *Sour Sweet.* **Octopus.** This is the story of a Chinese family in London in the 1960s. In addition to having a good plot the book gives insights into what the British culture and system look like to two sisters and their elderly father when he joins them from Hong Kong.

Chang, Jung. 1993. *Wild Swans: The Story of Three Daughters of China.* **Flamingo.** Chang tells the story of her grandmother, her mother and herself between 1909 and 1978 and, in the process, gives the reader an excellent history of twentieth-century China.

India and Pakistan

Chaudhuri, Nirad. 1987. *Thy Hand Great Anarch: India 1921–1952* **Chatto and Windus.** V.S. Naipaul describes this autobiography as 'the one great book to come out of the Indo-English encounter'. It covers his life as a clerk, broadcaster, and journalist at a crucial period in the history of India and the formation of Pakistan.

Wood, Heather. 1980. *Third Class Ticket.* **Routledge and Kegan Paul.** In 1969 a remarkable journey was made by 40 elderly Bengali villagers, an adventure made possible by a trust fund bequeathed by their land owner on her death. She had said 'I want my people to see India ... my village is a very small and poor one' (p. 3). The villagers made their journey and returned to the years of crisis in Bengal as the new state of Bangladesh was formed.

Wolpert, Stanley. 1993. *A New History of India.* **Oxford University Press.**

Large print

Isis large-print books and a new service, **Isis Reminiscence Services**, have been developed with the older reader in mind. For details about their publication contact their promotions department: **Isis Books Ltd, 55 St Thomas St, Oxford OX1 1JG. Tel: 0865 250333.** Large-print books are also available in public libraries.

History and general

Journal of Oral History, 247/249 Vauxhall Bridge Road, London SW1V 1HQ.

Mercer, D. ed. 1988. *Chronicle Of The 20th Century.* **Chronicle London.** An enormous reference book that details the history of the twentieth century month by month. It includes short articles on significant, amusing or amazing events.

Willis, Roy, ed. 1993. *World Mythology: The Illustrated Guide.* **Simon and Schuster.**

Video

The Variety Movie Guide. **1994. Hamlyn, £12.99.** Gives over 6500 reviews of 80 years of film.

Africa – The Rise of Nationalism and *The legacy*, **The Other Cinema, 79 Wardour St, London WIV 3TH.** Two videos, the former focuses on African independence struggles and the latter on the legacy of colonial rule for newly liberated states.

Library of Twentieth Century Newsreel, **WH Smith.** Three hours of British Movietone News.

The Very Best of Dad's Army. **BBC**.

The Best of British Cinema **series:** Song and Dance with George Formby and Gracie Fields, the Ealing Comedies and slapstick.

Parkfield Pathe. *A Year to Remember* **series.** Sixty minutes worth of newsreel for each year.

Quartet International Inc, Volumes 1–8: 1918–1939. *Between the Wars.*

CHAPTER 8

Cultural information, dates and events 1900–1990

This chapter lists some events of the twentieth century that will almost certainly have had an impact on the lives of the old people involved in reminiscence work. The dates and events that follow are not intended to be a potted history of this century but rather to act as a reminder that an important part of understanding an old person and their experiences is an understanding of the social and cultural context in which those values were formed. For this reason information about fashion, popular music and everyday life has also been included alongside world events. The events that are of the greatest importance to an 85-year-old woman or man may or may not have significance in world history. Listen to *them*: reminiscence is about telling *their* story; it is not a world history.

Old people, for example, may want to talk about evenings spent around the gramophone in the 1920s, be it in their Wiltshire village or in their home in New Amsterdam, Guiana [Guyana]. In this instance a knowledge of popular songs or hymns of the time is going to be the prime focus and not the Depression in Britain or the need to migrate from the West Indies to find work. Life sixty years ago may be more vivid to them than life now. It is easier to understand the texture and the quality of their memories if one sets them in a realistic context. The intensity of village life in the early part of the century is more easily understood if one appreciates the difficulties of travelling away from the village in a world without motor cars and with only a limited income. Without television or radio, people relied on each other for entertainment and company.

The information is arranged by decade, the dates and events listed for each decade with information on social, political and technological changes, fashion, popular music and culture at the beginning of each section. The dates and events are preceded by a small amount of background information on five ethnic minority groups and their home countries and cultures. The five are Hong Kong Chinese, Caribbeans, Pakistanis, Bangladeshis and Cypriots. All of these countries have been or are still British colonies and although culturally diverse they all have a common tie to Britain, the 'Mother Country', a tie that colonial rule fostered. This link is illustrated by M from Guyana: 'It was an advantage being brought up in Guyana as far as living in England was concerned. There was some common ground because Guyana had been a British colony and some of the old habits die hard. We used to have to learn a lot about Britain in school: British history, geography, etc. (Schweitzer, 1984, p. 29). In addition to being useful in their own right the five 'samples' will prove useful as a checklist of background information that should be collected before embarking on work with people whose culture and home country are unfamiliar. The local public library should be able to lend books that reflect the nature of the population of the area as libraries are required to have collections that reflect the nature and interests of the populations they serve. If it does not have what is needed in stock, it may be prepared to buy relevant books and will certainly have access to inter-library loans.

The 1991 census gave 32 categories of ethnicity; 5% of the population, that is, three million people, are from ethnic minorities, one of the largest ethnic groups being Black African [207,000]. There is no cultural information on Black Africans included in this chapter as there are many countries and cultures subsumed in the category 'Black African' and each of these needs to be explored and understood in its own right. Many of the national boundaries in Africa were created by Europeans and their governments as they colonised. These boundaries cut across natural communities and tribal territories. David Lamb's book *The Africans* (1984) gives a succinct overview of Africa's history including the colonial heritage, profiles of the different countries and their cultures.

ETHNIC GROUPS

Pakistan and Bangladesh

Pakistan and Bangladesh are two Asian nations situated on opposite sides of India. With India they form the huge landmass known as the Indian sub-continent.

Pakistan is the larger of the two and lies to the north-west of India. Excluding the territory of Kashmir which is in dispute with India it is the same size as France and Britain put together. Its neighbours are Iran, Afghanistan, China and India. Much of Persian or Iranian culture and language has been absorbed into Pakistan's own culture.

Bangladesh lies to the north-east of India. It is the same size as England and Northern Ireland combined and is roughly one-fifth the size of Pakistan.

Bangladesh has a population of 110 million, Pakistan of 120 million. The north of Pakistan is dominated by the Himalayan mountains. Much of Bangladesh lies below sea level and is liable to flooding. In the rainy season large parts of the country simply disappear under water. In Bangladesh the River Ganges meets the Brahmaputra and Jamuna rivers and forms the Padma, which in turn joins the Meghna; together they form an enormous delta known as the Mouth of the Ganges and this flows into the Bay of Bengal.

In Pakistan the Indus River and its tributaries the Jhelum, Chenab, Ravi and Sutlej, flow across Pakistan and the majority of the population live in the fertile areas surrounding the rivers. The monsoon or seasonal rains can be accompanied by cyclones. Whilst the Bangladeshis in particular are dependent on the monsoon rains for good rice and other crops, often the sudden increase in the amount of water causes severe flooding.

Archaeological evidence shows that Pakistan and Bangladesh were inhabited around 6,000 years ago. Early in history the Aryans arrived, probably coming from Iran. They gave the sub-continent its main religion, Hinduism. The Aryans were followed by the Arabs who brought with them Islam; Muslims, who follow Islam, take their name from the Prophet Muhammad.

The history of the Indian sub-continent is marked by invasion after invasion. The most famous and successful amongst these invaders were the Moguls who were still ruling in the seventeenth century when the British, French and other Europeans arrived in the sub-continent, initially to trade, and subsequently to take possession. The British gradually extended their control of the country fighting battles and displacing many local rulers. By the late nineteenth century the first Viceroy of India ruled the country on behalf of Queen Victoria, when she proclaimed herself Empress of India.

The Indian National League and the Muslim League were founded to represent the interests of local people. Freedom fighters like Jawaharlal Nehru, Muhammad Ali Jinnah and Mahatma Gandhi, emerged to lead what was mostly a peaceful struggle for home rule. Gandhi was the dominant Indian figure of this period. His political philosophy contained two messages: that Indians should restore economic self-sufficiency by reviving simple tasks (his symbol was a spinning wheel), and *satyagraha* – his belief that truth and justice will ultimately prevail if insisted on by peaceful pressure. In the 1930s the Muslim League started to express concern that the British might be replaced by Hindu rule and by 1940 its members were calling for the foundation of a separate Muslim state.

When the British finally left in 1947 they left the sub-continent divided into two independent states, India and Pakistan, a process known as Partition. In 1947, a quarter of India and Pakistan including Kashmir was still comprised of princely states, ruled by dynastic families. The Portuguese continued to hold Goa until 1961 when the Indian troops took it from them. Pakistan comprised two areas, what we know today as Bangladesh and Pakistan. In both, Muslims were the majority. Many Muslims migrated from India to Pakistan, as Hindus and Sikhs migrated from Pakistan to India. Nevertheless, many stayed put and today there are as many Muslims in India as there are in Pakistan or Bangladesh. Partition resulted in hundreds of thousands of refugees and many people being massacred. Salman Rushdie in *Midnight's Children* (1982, p. 73) writes:

> The children had their own names for most of the local inhabitants. One group of three neighbours was known as the 'fighting cock people' because they comprised one Sindhi and one Bengali householder whose homes were separated by one of the few Hindu residences. The Sindhi and the Bengali had very little in common – they didn't speak the same language or cook the same food; but they were both Muslim and they both detested the interposed Hindu.

Pakistan, as a new nation, had many problems. Its territory was split. The old capital had been Delhi and that was in India. By 1958 martial law was imposed. Resentment grew in what was to become Bangladesh and finally erupted in the early 1970s. The Indian army joined in on the side of Bangladesh. The war was short but bloody and the sub-continent was partitioned for the second time with Bangladesh becoming a separate country. When Bangladesh was welcomed into the British Commonwealth, Pakistan was so deeply offended that it withdrew from the Commonwealth, although it has rejoined since.

Ninety-eight per cent of Bangladeshis are Bengali. Many migrate to the neighbouring Indian states of Assam and Tripura in search of work. For the same reasons many Bangladeshis have settled in the Middle East and Britain. Most of the Bangladeshis in Britain have come from the Sylhet region of East Bangladesh.

Bengali, the language of Bangladesh and of India's West Bengal state, is based on Sanskrit and is written from left to right. It is the native tongue of more than 150 million people. It is a language much used in films. Author Rabindranath Tagore made a major contribution to establishing Bengali as a literary language. Urdu, the national language of Pakistan, is written from right to left. It has been strongly influenced by Persian. Few Pakistanis would speak Urdu as their first language but it is considered the first language of Islam and around 50 million people speak it.

Around 68% of Pakistanis and 78% of Bangladeshis live in the countryside. City dwellers tend to be much better off than country dwellers. Many men leave the countryside to seek work in the cities and often end up living in shanty towns on the outskirts of the city.

Village dwellings are made of cane, wood and possibly mud. Water needs to be carried from a well or pump. Both Pakistan and Bangladesh are essentially farming countries. The size of the population and its tendency to flood makes for a constant struggle in Bangladesh. Key crops in Bangladesh are jute, tea, and prawns and shrimps.

Though Muslims do not eat pork, they do eat meat – beef, goat or buffalo, chicken is also popular. Rice and wheat – made into chapattis – are staples. Jackfruit, bananas, oranges and papayas are grown and eaten in both countries. Alcoholic drink is forbidden by Islam.

Muslims are expected to pray several times a day and the *muezzin* or mosque official calls them to prayer, usually over a loudspeaker. Strict Muslim countries expect women to remain in purdah – out of sight of all men except their husbands. City dwellers in Pakistan are not particularly strict about this but it is common in the villages and the countryside. In both Bangladesh and Pakistan, Friday is observed as the day of rest and prayer.

Hong Kong Chinese

The overwhelming majority of elderly Chinese people in Britain will have come from Hong Kong.

Hong Kong is a British colony, due to be handed back to the Chinese in 1997. Jan Morris' book *Hong Kong: Epilogue to an Empire* (1990) gives an excellent history of the territory. Hong Kong comprises over 230 islands, including Hong Kong Island itself and a peninsula of mainland China, which is made up of Kowloon and the New Territories. The majority of people live in high-rise apartments on Hong Kong Island, in Kowloon or one of the towns in the New Territories. However, a significant minority of people do live on the outlying islands or on their fishing boats.

Chinese has one written language and many dialects. Most Hong Kong people speak the Cantonese dialect, although the indigenous Chinese populations of the area, the Tanka, Hoklo and Hakka, speak their own dialects.

The climate in Hong Kong varies from an average of 30°C in the summer to 18–20°C in the winter. Eighty per cent of the annual rainfall falls in the summer. Hong Kong has in the past suffered from severe water shortages and water rationing, at times four hours' water supply every other day. However, since relations with China have relaxed, water is now supplied from China and water rationing no longer occurs. About thirty or so tropical cyclones form in the seas around Hong Kong each year, half of these reaching the high speeds of a typhoon. The word 'typhoon' derives from the Cantonese *tai fung* [big wind]. Wind speeds can get up to 150 knots accompanied by heavy rain fall. The damage they cause can be enormous, and living through them, be it in a village house, fishing boat or twenty-third-floor apartment, can be extremely frightening. In one of the worst typhoons, in 1937, 1000 small boats were lost and 2500 people killed.

Hong Kong was a well established trading centre by the 1920s and 30s, having been a British colony since 1841. Civil wars in China in the 1920s and 1930s meant that many people fled to Hong Kong for safety. In December 1941, however, the Japanese invaded Hong Kong and held it throughout the Second World War. The British who were left in Hong Kong were almost all interned as prisoners of war, where conditions were difficult but not as difficult as the conditions endured by the Chinese people, who were not interned. Many people have appalling stories of hardship to tell, and still resent the Japanese. Some families sent their children and young people away to the extended family in mainland China or to Macau, the small Portuguese colony along the Chinese coast, which remained neutral during the war. In August 1945 the war ended and the Hong Kong economy gradually got going again, helped initially by the 'Dollar a Day' scheme, where the government paid anyone a dollar a day to help clear up the devastation left by the occupation.

In 1949 the Communists seized power in China and an estimated 750 000 people fled to Hong Kong to escape the new regime. Large numbers of these people lived in shanty towns on the Hong Kong hillsides, in shacks made out of bamboo, corrugated iron and other found materials; there was no sanitation and they collected water from standpipes. The Hong Kong government began an aggressive building and rehousing programme. The programme has meant that the Hong Kong government has now become the world's largest landlord, with almost half of the population of Hong Kong living in government housing. The resettlement housing that the government built was very basic and the apartments offered to families (often comprising three generations) were only one room, with bathroom and kitchen facilities shared with five or six other families.

Immigrants continued to pour into crowded Hong Kong from mainland China. During the 1960s the government operated an immigration policy called 'touch base' and any immigrant who could touch base with friends or relatives and make it to register in the town centre could stay. Those who could not or who were caught on the border or before they had touched base were sent back. During the 1960s and 1970s about a third of immigrants were sent back. By 1980 there were 3500 illegal immigrants coming in a day. In an attempt to control immigration, the government introduced ID cards for Hong

Kong citizens and anyone without an ID card was deported. Today some 55 000 legal migrants arrive each year. Hong Kong's population is now six million, compared with 880 000 in the 1930s.

Chinese people work to two calendars, the western 12-month calendar and the lunar 13-month calendar. The dates of the religious festivals and of Chinese New Year are determined by the lunar calendar. Good luck is extremely important to the Chinese who are a very superstitious people. People go to great lengths to ensure good luck. Buildings must be built in the best place and the *fung-shui* [the influences of wind-water] must be right. Even today, professional geomancers are employed to ensure modern buildings have good *fung-shui*. Chinese religion comprises a mixture of Taoism, Confucianism and Buddhism. Most Chinese people worship gods from all these religions and sometimes other gods as well. Tin Hau, goddess queen of the sea, is very popular; she protects fishermen amongst others. There are many temples dedicated to Tin Hau and she has her own festival. Ancestors are also extremely important to Chinese people and much revered. The annual festival of Ching Ming is a time when families travel often long distances to their ancestral villages, many in mainland China, to visit and spring clean the graves of their ancestors, and to leave offerings of food and wine.

Chinese people say that Cantonese people, including those in Hong Kong, will eat anything with wings except an aeroplane, anything with four legs except a table, and anything with three legs except a stool! Cantonese cooking is 'wet' on the whole with lots of gravy. It includes delicacies lost on the western palate such as chicken's claws, ducks' feet and gizzards and fishs' maw.

> The food here is very different . . . It may have something to do with the different growing methods we use. We fertilize our crops with nightsoil. The British can't stand the bad smell and discard it. They use chemicals instead. So the vegetables they grow are not as good tasting as ours. We don't eat foods that are out of season. We only eat what is fresh from the market and we don't freeze our food. The food is very different here. (W from Hong Kong, in Schweitzer, 1984, p. 20).

The Caribbean and the West Indies

The Caribbean takes its name from the Carib people, one of the tribes that were indigenous to the area. However, unlike the Carib, the majority of Caribbean peoples are of immigrant stock, either because their forebears were taken from Africa to the Caribbean as slaves or because after the abolition of slavery in 1834 their forebears came to work as cheap or indentured labour. The majority of these labourers came from India, China or Japan. Indentured labour provided plantation owners with a cheap alternative to slaves after slavery was abolished. Indentured labourers worked for only food, in order to recompense employers for the cost of their passage. Indentureship was finally abolished in 1917, largely due to the efforts of Gandhi who was deeply concerned about indentured labour in Mauritius, South Africa, Fiji and the West Indies. Slaves were brought mainly from Ghana and other parts of the west coast of Africa. There are also white people who regard the West Indies as their home. Although the majority of them are well-off – in 1969 in Jamaica, 0.02% of the population, that is 330 whites, owned 50% of the land – there is a significant minority of poor whites, notably in Barbados and St Thomas.

The West Indies comprises a 4000 km long archipelago in the Caribbean Sea and some countries on the American coast. There are three main groups of islands: the Bahamas, the Lesser Antilles and the Greater Antilles. There are thousands of islands in the West Indies and the landscape and geography varies from island to island. Grenada, Dominica, Guadeloupe, Monserrat and eastern Jamaica are all ruggedly mountainous, whilst Barbados, Antigua and western Jamaica are flat. The climate is magnificent, marred only by the hurricane season in the late summer and autumn. Hurricanes can be extremely destructive: the city of Belize was destroyed by a hurricane in 1931. Vivid colours both on land and under water characterise the West Indies. Derek Walcott, the Nobel-Prize-winning poet, has said that his work owes its strength and intensity to growing up in St Lucia.

The Spanish, French, British, Dutch, and even the Danes had colonies in the West Indies. Although many countries in the West Indies have natural mineral resources and manufacturing potential, the colonial powers were not interested in developing these. They preferred to develop their colonies to provide resources for the 'Mother Country' and required colonies to produce goods that would supplement, but not compete with, their home economies. For example, Britain insisted that Monserrat's major crops were sugar, ginger, limes and cotton. Since becoming independent, mainly in the 1960s, West Indian countries have embarked on the diversification of agriculture and the development of manufacturing.

The main language spoken in each country would be that of the colonial power, with other languages both European and African mixed in. Anglophone or Commonwealth Caribbean is spoken in the Bahamas, the Turks and Caicos Islands, the Cayman Islands, Jamaica, Belize, the British Virgin Islands, Antigua and Barbuda, Anguilla, Monserrat, Dominica, St Lucia, St Vincent, St Kitts (St Christopher) and Nevis, Barbados, Grenada, Trinidad and Tobago and Guyana. In Jamaica, however, it is the second language to Jamaican dialect, a dialect that mixes English, Spanish and various African languages, the most dominant of these being Twi from Ghana. Tales and folklore were largely responsible for keeping the African languages alive. The legendary Jamaican spider Anansi, a great survivor due largely to his own wit and cunning, has his origins in Upper Guinea, West Africa.

Religious occasions and festivals draw from Anglican and Roman Catholic Christian traditions combined with African religions and beliefs, and belief in magic powers, for example, in *pocomania* in Jamaica or *vodou* (voodoo) in Haiti. Sundays and attending church are important to many West Indians and people coming to Britain were shocked at how few people in Britain went to church on Sundays. People of Indian origin have retained their Hindu faith. Rastafarianism, started in Jamaica in the 1920s, is based on the Bible and in particular the Old Testament and the Book of Revelation. It places emphasis on eating organic food that is not processed. Rastafarians were motivated by the teachings of Marcus Garvey, the founder of The Universal Negro Improvement Association. They regard Ras Tafari (Haile Salassie), once Emperor of Ethiopia, as the living God. They believe that salvation for people of African descent can only be found in Africa – 'Babylon' – and that their adopted countries will eventually be destroyed.

People shop at open-air markets across the West Indies. Traditionally, it is the women who take the goods to market. Country people travel for hours often by bus or on foot to get there. Fish, often dried or salted, pork and goat are eaten, as are local fruit and vegetables, as M from Guyana describes:

> In the yard we had pigeon peas, ochras, boulange mangoes, star apples, custard apples, sapodilla and papaya ... My favourite meal was metagee. The main vegetables [are] plantains, cassava, sweet potatoes – you have to be careful to add the potatoes when it is nearly finished. You put the plantain at the bottom. Then you grate the coconut and squeeze the milk through a linen cloth over the vegetables. When the plantain at the bottom begins to burn you mix your duff and add it. If you have it you can put dried fish or meat into steam. Oh we children used to fight for the bottom of the pot! (Schweitzer, 1984, p. 29).

In 1945 a British Government report looked at conditions in Jamaica, the Leeward Islands, the Windward Islands, Barbados, Trinidad and Tobago, British Honduras and British Guiana. It found 'poor housing, poor wages, chronic sickness and an education system with serious inadequacies'. The majority of schools and clinics and hospitals had been provided by Christian missionaries. Although Barbados had been a British colony since 1625 it was only in 1961, five years before independence, that free secondary education was introduced.

Cyprus

Cyprus, because of its location, has a long international history, having been inhabited and occupied by, amongst others, the Romans, the Venetians, the Turkish Ottoman Empire and the British. Today the island is divided between Greek and Turkish Cypriots. In 1878 Britain took over Cyprus from the Ottoman Empire and paid the Sultan an annual tribute equal to the amount of profit Cyprus would have yielded him. In 1915 Britain offered Cyprus to Greece in an attempt to get Greece to enter the First World War. Greece did not accept.

During its rule, Britain established a new legal system based on English legal procedures and a legislative council – a rudimentary parliament. It improved educational facilities, afforested areas, controlled locusts, reduced crime and the incidence of malaria. It built 3000 miles of roads, and irrigation systems and water supplies. However, in common with its behaviour in all its colonies, Britain did not fulfil its promise to make Cyprus highly prosperous and productive; Cyprus was there to provide Britain with a miltary base and goods, as and when required. The stability that British rule brought allowed the population to increase and by 1921 there were 246 500 Cypriots and 470 British inhabitants, and income per capita and standards of living rose. However the Greek Cypriots remained unhappy with British rule and this erupted into serious rioting in 1931. It was not until 1947 that *enosis* – self-determination – became a serious possibility for Cyprus. In 1947 the Cypriots rejected the British offer to make a constitution; in 1950 Bishop, later Archbishop, Makarios organised a plebiscite in which 96% of the population voted in favour of *enosis*. Lawrence Durrell's book *Bitter Lemons of Cyprus* (1957) gives an excellent description of life in Cyprus at that time.

The Turkish government acknowledged that Cyprus was British. They and the Greek government accepted Britain's offer to join talks to discuss Cyprus' future. By accepting, the Greek government tacitly acknowledged the Turkish government's rights over Cyprus. Those talks failed and negotiation continued until British rule ended in 1960. The Treaty of Zurich that established Cyprus as a republic agreed that Britain could retain sovereignty over its military bases, and that Cyprus would become a unitary state with a Greek Cypriot president and a Turkish Cypriot vice-president, the vice-president having a right of veto on security and external policy. It was then that the Turks claimed 30% of Cyprus, although Turks only made up 17% of the population. Violence followed the creation of the republic. In 1964 the UN sent in a peace-keeping force that has been there ever since. In 1974 the mainland Greek military junta attempted to depose Archbishop Makarios. The attempt failed and in addition it resulted in the Turkish government launching an offensive. Cyprus was divided and Turks fled to the north of the island, Greeks to the south. Property was abandoned, mosques and churches boarded up, and they still stand empty today.

> Since the Turkish invasion of 1974, the population had drastically polarised. The Greek Cypriots – some eighty percent of the inhabitants – have crowded into the southern part of the island, while the Turkish Cypriots occupy the north. It is an unhappy and unequal division ... The nervous co-habitation which I witnessed in 1972 was, I realise, the island's halycon time – and this [book] is a record of a country which will not return. (Thubron, 1986, preface, p. vi)

Different parts of Cyprus vary physically:

> I had already begun to see the island as a whole, building my picture of it from the conversations of my host. With him I had spent three winters snowed up on Troodos, [Cyprus's central mountain range] teaching in a village school so cold that the children's teeth chattered as they wrote; with him I panted and sweated in the ferocious August heat of the plains; suffered from malaria at Larnaca; spent holidays amongst the rolling vineyards of Paphos in search of vines to transplant; like him I always came back to the Kyrenia range, to cool my mind and gladden my heart with its greenness, its carpets of wild anemones, its castles and monasteries. (Durrell, 1957, pp. 31–32)

Many people lived off the land and lived very simply:

> I was used to these houses by now: the few bare rooms, the iron beds, ungainly wardrobes, mantlepieces garnished with cheap china and plastic flowers; the shock of an enormous washing machine. On the wall Loizos' [his host] parents dressed and waistcoated in old peasant robes looked out from the one photograph of their lives, as from a state portrait, his hair parted at the middle in two scrupulously glossy waves. Their faces were faded as if gazing from some far older time (Thubron, p. 105)

Life was often hard for children:

> My mother died when I was three years old, my father was a shepherd in Cyprus. I went to school when I was seven and left when I was ten years old. I started work with my father looking after the animals. He did not have any aspirations for me as it was the done thing to go and help with the job your parents are doing. (GW in Schweitzer, 1984, p. 10)

As in many peasant cultures water was often at a premium:

Water is so scarce in Cyprus that it is sold in parcels. You buy an hour here and an hour there from the owner of a spring ... The water rights form part of the property titles of citizens and are divided up on the death of the owner among his dependants ... Families being what they are it is common for a single spring to be owned by upwards of thirty people. (Durrell, 1957, p. 61)

Thubron (1986, p. 134) describes a typical meal that a peasant family who put him up served to him:

She had prepared a supper of every food in the house: eggs, artichokes and cucumbers, lamb and fried haloumi [cheese] and 'bullybeef' – the word had passed into Greek – with mounds of peas and fruit.

DATES AND EVENTS

The following list of dates and events and descriptions gives an overview of what was happening in different parts of the world and when. For more detail about specific years use the books and videos listed in Chapter 7.

1900–1909

The world map looked very different then. Britain, France and Germany ruled many countries as part of their empires. When Queen Victoria died in 1901 she had reigned for 63 years, ruling both Britain and an empire 'on which the sun never set'.

Britain also influenced life in countries it did not rule; this influence was mainly due to the machines and manufacturing ability that the industrial revolution had created, machines and abilities which other nations wanted to buy or own.

In Britain conditions were poor for working people. They had outside toilets, bathrooms and running water were a luxury. Lighting was provided by gas or oil lamps, heating and cooking on coal or wood fires, washing by hand in a tub. Many people worked long hours for low wages in bad conditions. When people were unable to support themselves financially, they turned to the state or charity for help. The government wanted to discourage this and made distinctions between the 'deserving' and the 'undeserving' poor and only the deserving poor got help. Old people would be sent to the workhouse, where men and women had to live separately. They slept in dormitories and their diet was restricted. Children who were orphans or whose families could not support them were sent to orphanages such as Dr Barnardo's Homes for Waifs and Strays (now Barnardo's). People with mental illnesses or handicaps were incarcerated in large prison-like hospitals. In 1904, 25 000 people lived in workhouses and 520 were getting 'outdoor relief', that is, food or small amounts of cash.

A woman's place was very definitely in the home. Women were seen as the weaker sex, dependent on men, and not responsible enough to have the vote, a view vigorously disputed by the women of the Suffragette Movement. The middle classes and the rich employed servants to enable them to live comfortably, running a household took a lot of time and energy.

Sunday was important as a day of rest and the majority of the population went to church.

People made their own entertainment at home. Popular songs were sold as sheet music although gramophones were starting to become popular with those who could afford them.

Cars started to appear on the roads; the 'Tin Lizzy', the Model T Ford, the first car that was affordable by those other than the very rich, went on sale in the USA in 1908.

1900	China	The Boxer Rebellion. This anti-Western up-rising failed and led to China being carved up into European 'areas of influence'.
1901	Britain	Queen Victoria dies.
	India	1.25 million people died in a famine. Britain blames over-population.
1905		Former USSR Revolution starts.
1906	Britain	Eleven suffragettes are jailed after protesting that women should have the vote.
1907	West Indies	An earthquake devastates Kingston, Jamaica. The British Governor rejects aid from the US fleet but later accepts help from British ships.
1909	Britain	First pensions are paid out at the Post Office. People over 70 got 5 shillings (12½p), 7 shillings and 6 pence (37p) for a married couple. Some people were excluded from getting pensions. These included those who had failed to work to their ability, prisoners, the insane and paupers.

1910–1919

For Europe and the colonies of European countries, this decade was dominated by the Great War, the First World War 1914–1918. The war left 10 million dead, 750 000 of them British. 200 000 of these were soldiers from the British Empire, a third from the Indian Army. Under white officers, the Gold Coast Regiment (now Ghana), King's African Rifles and eight divisions of the British West Indies Regiment fought for Britain. One thousand black seamen from Cardiff died in the war. A poet recorded the men killed as 'The Lost Generation.'

In Ireland there was fighting and unrest over British rule, which climaxed in the Easter Uprising of 1916.

In China, the child emperor Pu Yi, (the subject of the film *The Last Emperor*) gave the country its first constitution, before resigning when a republic was established. Slavery and the castration of men to make a servant class of eunuchs was abolished.

In Russia civil war broke out, culminating in the Revolution and by the end of the decade the country was Communist.

In India, Gandhi led a call for independence from Britain.

In Britain, because of the war, women were needed to take over men's jobs on the land, in factories and offices, and as nurses at the front. This fuelled the resolve of the Suffragette Movement to fight for the vote for women. In 1918 women over 30 were allowed to vote for the first time and the first woman MP was elected.

Labour-saving devices were introduced. They included vacuum cleaners, electric irons, washing machines and electric fires. However they were expensive, a vacuum cleaner at £30 cost the equivalent of almost two years' old-age pension. They were therefore only used by wealthy households and servants had to be trained to use them. Electricity was seen as the power of the future.

Popular music of this decade included 'Keep the Home Fires Burning', 'Pack up Your Troubles in Your Old Kit Bag', 'Oh Oh Oh What A Lovely War'.

| 1910 | Britain | King Edward VII dies |
| | | 80 Labour Exchanges are opened and inundated with people looking for work. |

	Ireland	Carson, the leader of the Unionist MPs, declares that Ulster will fight against Home Rule for Ireland.
	South Africa	The Union of South Africa is formed.
1912	Britain	Suffragettes smash windows in West End shops; 120 are arrested.
		The ocean liner, SS *Titanic*, sinks on her first trans-Atlantic crossing; 1500 of the 2340 passengers and crew die.
	Ireland	Loyalists, loyal to Britain, pledge to fight against Home Rule for Ireland. There are queues three-quarters of a mile long outside Belfast City Hall waiting to sign a covenant confirming their opposition to Home Rule. Some sign in blood bringing razors and pins with them for that purpose.
	China	Pu Yi, the five-year-old Emperor of China, grants a constitution. Slavery is also abolished by Imperial Decree. Dr Sun Yat Sen proclaims a provisional government in the south and later becomes the first president of the Republic. The emperor resigns though he and the nobles are allowed to retain their titles.
	South Africa	The African National Congress is founded.
1913	Britain	Sickness benefit and maternity benefit are introduced.
1914	Europe	The First World War starts.
	West Indies	Jamaican Marcus Garvey founds the Universal Negro Improvement Association, which taught black people to have pride in themselves. It becomes a rallying point for nationalist movements that gave rise to the desire for full independence.
		The US occupies Haiti until 1934.
1915	Britain	Aliens are rounded up in Britain because of anti-German feeling. Women are urged to quit the home for the factory.
	Europe	At Gallipoli in the eastern Mediterranean, British, French and Anzac (Australian and New Zealand) troops are almost wiped out by the Turks. Anzac Day commemorates the bravery of those men.
1916	Europe	The Battle of the Somme and of Jutland.
	Ireland	In the Easter uprising in Dublin the 'rebels' seize control of the Post Office. The green,

white and orange tricolour flag is raised publicly for the first time. The brutality of the British suppression of the uprising leads to further inflamed feelings.

1917 Ireland Home rule is to exclude Ulster, Ireland is to be divided.

Former USSR Revolutions in Russia. The Bolsheviks seize control. the Tsar abdicates and is sent to Siberia with his family where they are massacred in 1918. This was the beginning of the Communist regime.

The US US enters the First World War to 'save democracy'.

1918 Europe The Allies break through the German lines; victory is celebrated by the Armistice.

Britain An influenza epidemic kills almost 750 000 people.

1919 Britain A British airship makes its first transatlantic trip. There is a general strike in Glasgow as the unions fight for a 40-hour week.

There are race riots over the employment of black people.

Ireland The partition of Ireland is planned.

India British troops kill and wound peaceful Sikh demonstrators in Amritsar.

Former USSR There is civil war.

The US Prohibition (of the sale and purchase of alcohol) starts.

1920–1929

Millions emigrated from Russia and Eastern Europe to Britain and America. Many of those going to America travelled via British ports. Few could speak English; many were Jews fleeing persecution.

Rastafarianism started in the West Indies.

In China, Dr Sun Yat Sen, the first president of the Republic, dies and in the virtual absence of a central government Chiang Kai Shek's Kuomintang movement attempts to take control in partnership with the small but influential Communist Party. In 1927 he purged the Communist Party, laying the basis for a feud that continued intermittently until 1949 when the Communists took over and what remained of the Kuomintang were killed, imprisoned or fled, many to Hong Kong or to Formosa (Taiwan).

In Britain there was widespread hunger and poverty and, in many areas, no work.

Cars, like the 1922 Morris Oxford and Morris Cowley, began to be available to ordinary people. Horses were still used on farms and in the country. Many people rode bicycles.

Public opinion felt skirts rose and morals declined as women developed a flat-chested look with short skirts and short hair, and both drank and smoked. Wide-legged trousers known as 'Oxford Bags' were the height of fashion for men.

In 1922 the BBC began broadcasting; cinema gradually became mass entertainment and many people went once or twice a week. Charlie Chaplin and Buster Keaton delighted cinema audiences with their films, like *The Gold Rush* (Chaplin), *The General* (Keaton).

Noel Coward's musical plays were popular.

Popular music of the decade included 'I Can't Give You Anything But Love', 'Old Man River', 'A Room With A View', 'Ain't She Sweet', 'Amongst My Souvenirs'.

1920	Britain	The government announces that it will build 100 000 new homes.
		The police get cars instead of horses.
		The miners strike, other transport workers threatening to join in.
		The 'wets' and 'drys' clash in Scotland. The wets being the whisky distillers, the drys, the non-conformist church. The drys' slogan 'Hell is a well of whisky' is met by a response from the wets 'Death where is thy Sting'.
	Ireland	The Ulster Unionists accept plans for an Ulster parliament. The Home Rule bill is passed. Riots in Belfast.
1921	Britain	The first birth-control clinic, Marie Stopes' Mothers' Clinic, opens to 'uproar'.
		2.2 million people are unemployed.
		On the fiftieth anniversary of the first bank holiday hundreds of thousands pack the seaside towns.

		Charlie Chaplin is mobbed as he returns to London.
	Ireland	British tanks patrol the streets of Dublin.
	India	Gandhi orders a boycott of the Prince of Wales' visit to Allahabad. Bombay riots as Gandhi burns foreign cloth as a protest.
	China	Sun Yat Sen becomes president.
	Canada	Insulin is discovered.
	Italy	Mussolini declares himself 'Il Duce' – the leader of the national fascist party.
1922	Britain	The BBC is formed and the first regular news broadcast is made. Most listeners use headphones, some have loud speakers.
	Ireland	An amnesty by the Irish government is given to all those who lay down their arms and surrender seized property. The Free State is declared.
	India	Gandhi is charged with sedition and given six years' imprisonment.
	China	Civil war between the north and south seems almost to come to an end.
1923	India	A tax on salt is reintroduced.
	Germany	Adolf Hitler stages a coup which fails. Inflation rises sharply.
	Turkey	Becomes a Republic under Ataturk.
1924	Britain	The Labour Party comes to power for the first time. Their first budget cuts 4d (2p) off a pound of tea, ½d (1/4p) off a pound of sugar. However, there is another election within the year which returns the Tories.
	India	Gandhi is released from prison.
	Former USSR	Lenin dies; Stalin takes control.
1925	Britain	Over the next ten years, half a million Britons will be encouraged to go to Australia. At the 1925 Motor Show a Rolls-Royce costs £1,891, a Jowett £150, a Citroen £145.
	China	Dr Sun Yat Sen dies. Chiang Kai Shek and the Kuomintang take control.
	Cyprus	Becomes a British colony having been annexed by the British in 1914 from Germany.
1926	Britain	Logie Baird transmits moving pictures by wireless – the first television. There is a general strike of all working people for better pay and conditions. The middle classes rally to beat the strike.

	India	Hindu and Muslim rioting.
	China	The Communist Red Army captures Canton in South China.
	Australia Canada New Zealand South Africa	Become Dominions remaining within the British Commonwealth but are no longer part of the Empire.
1927	Britain	Two hundred Welsh miners arrive in London after walking 180 miles, seeking work. There is a white Christmas with freezing blizzards. Food is dropped from the air into villages that are cut off.
	China	Chiang Kai-Shek and the Kuomintang unify most of China.
1928	Britain	The Thames bursts its bank; 14 are drowned.
	India	Indian nationalists do not want India to be a colony but rather to have Dominion status within the Commonwealth.
	Former USSR	Stalin's first Five-Year-Plan to increase agricultural and industrial production starts.
	The US	The 'talkies' (talking pictures) are here to stay says Hollywood.
1929	Britain	The air-mail letter service is established. The first 15 000 letters from India arrive two minutes early at Croydon. Traffic lights are used as an experiment in Oxford Street in London. The Labour Party is returned to power.
	India	Gandhi is elected as president of the Indian National Congress but will not accept the post. The longest electrified railway in the Empire, 116 miles, is opened from Bombay to Poona.
	The US	The stock market on Wall Street crashes, many people lose all their money.

1930–1939

Europe lived in the shadow of what became the Second World War in 1939. As Hitler's power grew and life became more and more difficult for Jews from Germany and Holland, they escaped to Britain and the US.

Although in China civil war continued, the invasion by the Japanese towards the end of the decade caused bombing, carnage and bloodshed on a far greater scale.

The Middle East and the Balkans were in turmoil.

Troubles continued in India (British India that is, not the Princely States) which gained provisional self-government in 1935.

Rioting and strikes in the West Indies were fuelled by poor housing and unemployment. Britain ordered a Royal Commission to investigate.

In Britain unemployment reached a record three million. Whilst many people continued to live in poverty, many others enjoyed a rising standard of living with cars, radios, holidays and new homes. A house in Mill Hill, North London, cost around £800. In Sainsbury's tea was 10d (4p), 1 dozen eggs 1 shilling (5p), 1lb of butter 1 shilling (5p). By 1939 tinned food and plastics were widely available. Medical treatment was aided by the use of X-rays. Pierced ears became fashionable. Women over 21 gained the right to vote.

People took Sunday afternoon drives in the country, or took train excursions or went hiking. British Rail and London Underground produced posters encouraging such activities, posters which have been reproduced today either full-size or postcard size.

Noel Coward's *Private Lives* was on stage in the West End of London. Cinema was very popular. Hollywood produced ever increasing numbers of films, with sound quality improving. When Walt Disney's *Snow White and the Seven Dwarfs* was shown in Britain it got an A (adult) certificate from the film censors.

Popular music included: 'The Way You Look Tonight', 'When I'm Cleaning Windows', 'On the Sunny Side of the Street', 'Stormy Weather', 'Smoke Gets in Your Eyes', 'Who's Afraid of the Big Bad Wolf', 'I Only Have Eyes for You'. Gracie Fields was popular singing 'The Isle of Capri'.

1930	Britain	Unemployment is very high.
	India	Gandhi prepares to die in protest at the salt tax and marches with followers to the Bay of Cambay to make his own salt from the ocean. Violence continues during the year and Gandhi is imprisoned.

In London Indian delegates at round table talks pledge full equality to untouchables, the lowest caste in Indian society.

1931	Britain	Sir Oswald Mosley founds a new party, the party of Vitality and Manhood whose activists, who are Nazi supporters, will later become known as the 'blackshirts'.
		Sunday cinema becomes legal.
		The first trolley buses are introduced to London.
	India	Gandhi meets George V and Queen Mary in his loin-cloth.
	China	The Japanese occupy Manchuria.
1932	Ireland	Nationalist De Valera becomes prime minister.
	India	Has its first test match at Lord's versus England.
		Gandhi is on hunger strike in Poona jail. Britain says it will release Gandhi and 28 000 other prisoners.
	Germany	Hitler takes over as Chancellor of the German Reich.
		He orders a boycott of Jews and Jewish shops. Around 45 000 Jews are held in concentration camps.
	Former USSR	Widespread famine.
1933	The US	Prohibition ends.
1934	Britain	The Mersey Tunnel, the world's longest underwater tunnel, linking Liverpool with Birkenhead, is opened by the King.
		Five hundred hunger marchers reach London from Glasgow.
		Prime Minister Ramsay MacDonald refuses to see them.
	Germany	Hitler says the Third Reich will last a thousand years.
		German Nazis murder the Austrian Chancellor.
1935	Britain	King George V's Silver Jubilee is celebrated by street parties throughout Britain.
	India	British troops open fire on a huge crowd of Muslims who are rioting against Hindus, 27 are killed.
	China	Mao Tse Tung emerges as the Communist leader as his troops and supporters complete the Long March of 6000 miles despite clashes with Kuomintang and warlords. It is reckoned 100 000

perished during the march; only 30 000 arrived at their destination.

1936 Britain
Jobless people from Jarrow march to London to demand work.

Edward VIII abdicates saying 'I have found it impossible to carry the heavy burden of responsibility and discharge my duties as King as I would wish to do, without the help and support of the woman I love ... God bless you all. God Save the King.'

The Crystal Palace, built in 1851, burns down.

Germany
The Olympics are held in Berlin. Jesse Owens the black US runner wins the 200 metres event; Hitler refuses to shake his hand and leaves the stadium because Owens is black.

1937 Britain
The Duke of Windsor weds Wallis Simpson, the woman for whom he abdicated in 1936.

George VI, his younger brother, is crowned, with his Queen Elizabeth.

Ireland
The Free State is renamed Eire.

China
The Japanese invade and occupy Peking (Beijing).

Foreigners are evacuated from Shanghai. The Japanese overrun and bomb Shanghai.

The Communists and Kuomintang agree to make a united front against the Japanese.

The US
The *Hindenburg* airship explodes; 33 passengers and crew die. The explosion is recorded live by a radio commentator who weeps on air as he broadcasts.

Spain
Civil war. Hitler helps General Franco, leader of the fascists.

1938 Britain
Neville Chamberlain returns from Germany to tell the British people that he believes he had secured 'peace for our time'. In September, Chamberlain is party to negotiations for no war in Czechoslovakia with Mussolini, Hitler and Goering. In October, the Germans march into Czechoslovakia.

China
The Japanese arny bombs and occupies Canton (Guangzhou), in South China.

Austria
The Austrian people cheer as Hitler marches in.

1939 Europe
War is declared.

Britain	The Commonwealth sides with Britain, and troops are mobilised throughout the Commonwealth. One hundred thousand black personnel serve in the forces.
	Free air-raid shelters are delivered to London homes.
	Lights are blacked out in London's West End. Britain 'digs for victory': people are encouraged to grow their own vegetables.
	All moveable treasures are taken from London museums and galleries and Westminster Abbey to be hidden.
	One-and-half million children are evacuated from cities to the countryside and overseas, where it is thought they will be safer.
Germany	Jews are banned from becoming dentists, vets, pharmacists, from driving and from going to cinemas, the theatre or concerts.
	All women under 25 are required to do a year's civilian service for Hitler's Third Reich.
	Germany and Russia invade Poland.
Ireland	Remains neutral.
The US	Remains neutral.

1940–1949

This decade was dominated by the Second World War in Europe and in the Far East. It was only at the end of the war that the scale of Hitler's atrocities was revealed.

In addition to contributing to the war effort by sending troops, back at home, West Indian women knitted warm clothing for the troops, and even sent an ambulance to help. Despite their commitment to Britain and the war effort some experienced discrimination: a West Indian girl serving in the army in Britain was told 'You don't need shoes, at home you don't wear them anyway (Harriott, 1991, p. 32).

In China the war against the Japanese was followed by a civil war and many fled to Hong Kong or Formosa (Taiwan).

In Britain after the war a Labour Government was elected. It committed itself to rebuilding Britain. It nationalised major industries including coal, power and the railways. The Welfare State and National Health Service were born. Everyone now had the right to medical services free at the point of delivery and to secondary education, a state pension and other welfare benefits. Life was hard for most people even after the war ended as rationing of food and petrol continued.

In 1949 Prime Minister Winston Churchill visited Jamaica to appeal for workers to come to Britain.

Big band music was popular. Glenn Miller and his band toured to entertain the troops until the plane they were travelling in was lost over the English Channel.

Much Binding in the Marsh and *ITMA ('It's That Man Again')* with Tommy Handley and Co. were popular on radio as were *Dick Barton Special Agent* and *Woman's Hour*.

Laurence Olivier's film *Henry V* was widely acclaimed and his film of *Hamlet* won many awards. Orson Welles' film of Graham Greene's novel *The Third Man* gave an almost larger-than-life picture of life in Europe just after the war and the world of espionage.

Popular musical included: 'Marzy Doats', 'There Goes That Song Again', 'A Nightingale Sang in Berkeley Square', 'Whispering Grass', 'Buttons and Bows', 'Baby It's Cold Outside', 'Maybe It's Because I'm a Londoner', 'White Christmas', 'We'll Meet Again'.

1940	Britain	Two million people aged 19–27 are called up to the armed forces. The Thames freezes for the first time since 1888. The worst storms in living memory lash Britain. Food rationing is introduced. Churchill becomes Prime Minister. The Battle of Britain is fought between the Luftwaffe and the RAF in the height of summer. British cities are intensively bombed by the Germans; this includes Southampton which endures seven hours of continuous bombing and Coventry, devastated by a night of bombs. Many Londoners sleep in the Underground stations for safety. Princess Elizabeth, who later becomes Queen Elizabeth II, makes her first radio broadcast.
	France	The Germans take Boulogne. The Allies are evacuated from Dunkirk. The Germans take Paris and the French government signs an armistice with the Germans.

		French leader General De Gaulle says that the flame of French resistance must not go out.
	Poland	350 000 Jews are held in a ghetto.
		French Indo-China (Far East) is occupied by Japan
1941	Britain	Coal rationing is introduced.
	Far East	The Japanese bomb Pearl Harbor.
		Hong Kong falls to the Japanese on Christmas Day.
	Former USSR	Is invaded by Germany.
1942	Britain	Bells ring across Britain for the British victory against the Germans in North Africa at El Alamein.
	India	The Indian National Working Committee reject British plans for the future of India.
	Australia	The Japanese bomb the cities of Sydney and Newcastle.
	Far East	Singapore, Malaya [Malaysia] and the Philippines are taken by Japan.
	The US	Joins the war on the side of the Allies.
		Fights Japan in the Battles of the Coral Sea and Midway.
1943	Britain	Only blue or grey school uniforms are allowed in order to save on dye. Shoes are rationed to three pairs a year.
		Women's fashions encourage bare-leg patriotism, that is, not to wear stockings, but perhaps to paint a fake stocking seam up the back of the leg.
		Women no longer required to wear hats in the Church of England.
		The government declares all women are to do part-time work.
	Germany	The city of Hamburg is devastated by RAF bombing. The Germans are defeated at Stalingrad. This is the turning point of the war.
	Italy	Signs an armistice after defeat by the Allies.
1944	Britain	With the end of the war in sight the Allies increase the offensive against Germany and Japan.
		German V2 long-range rockets hit London with devastating results.
	France	D-Day: the Allies invade France, landing in Normandy.
		French tanks lead the Allies into Paris.

	Germany	Twenty million Germans are homeless after Allied bombing.
	Greece	Civil war breaks out.
	Burma	The Allies, mainly British and Indian troops, arrive by glider to go to occupied Burma's aid.
1945	Europe and the Far East	World War II ends. Fifty-five million have been killed.
	Britain	Victory is celebrated: VE day, Victory in Europe; VJ day, Victory over Japan. The lights are on in London, Piccadilly and the Strand for the first time in five years. The Labour Party have a landslide victory in the general election.
	Germany	Hitler kills himself. Russian troops occupy Berlin. The truth about the concentration camps is revealed. The Nuremburg trials start.
	Italy	Mussolini is shot dead.
	Hong Kong and Singapore	Are liberated from Japanese occupation.
	Japan	The atom bomb is dropped on Hiroshima and Nagasaki.
	Korea	Is divided, the Soviet-supported Peoples' Democratic Republic governing the North and the American-backed Republic of Korea controlling the South.
	Former USSR	In Yalta, Roosevelt, Churchill and Stalin carve up the post-war world.
1946	Britain	The first bananas arrive since before the war. The UK black market flourishes.
	India	Muslims and Hindus talk with a British cabinet delegation over the future of India. Thousands die in riots.
	China	The Kuomintang and Communist civil war starts, ending with the Kuomintang defeated.
	Israel	Jewish terrorists make many attacks in Palestine.
1947	Britain	Food is still rationed. The worst winter ever recorded is experienced – 300 roads are blocked, 15 towns cut off.
	India	The partition of India is agreed. Four hundred thousand die in the process and a further hundred thousand suffer from starvation and exposure. West and East Pakistan are

		separated from India. (East Pakistan is now known as Bangladesh.) The two Pakistans are mainly Muslim, with people of other religions staying on or returning to India. Partition results in 8 500 000 refugees: 2 300 000 travelling by train, the rest by bullock-cart or on foot.
	Israel	The situation in Palestine deteriorates and Israel declares itself an independent state.
1948	Britain	Half of Britain's doctors agree to join the new National Health Service.
		The GCE (General Certificate in Education) exam replaces the School Certificate and Higher School Certificate.
	India	Gandhi is shot dead.
	West Indies	The SS *Empire Windrush* brings 492 Jamaican job seekers to Britain. Most settle initially in Brixton.
1949	The USA	Sickle-cell anaemia is discovered.
	China	The Communist Party seizes power.
		Chiang Kai-Shek flees to Taiwan.

1950–1959

In Europe and the US youth culture dominated. Britain had some five million self-styled 'teenagers' who adopted their own style of dress: teddy boys wore the drape shape and girls wore stiletto heels. They met in coffee bars and had money to spend. The jive was popular. Bill Haley and his Comets made a popular tour of Britain. Elvis Presley became a teenage idol. There was concern amongst the older generation about his effect on the morals of young people; because of the way he moved and behaved on stage, people called him 'Elvis the Pelvis'.

In Britain, *The Goon Show* on the BBC Home Service became almost a cult, influencing comedy in the decades to follow. Hit records included 'Rock Around The Clock', 'Fly Me To The Moon' and 'Take Me Back To The Black Hills of Dakota'. Cinema audiences declined, and cinemas and theatres closed as television became more popular. The 1950s edition of *Mrs Beeton's Household Management* gives advice on and menus for a television viewing party!

The Far East was unsettled. In Korea there was war between the communist north and the south; Australia, Britain and the U.S. fought on the side of the south. There was war in Indo-China (1949–54) when the French sustained a humiliating defeat at the hands of Ho Chi Minh after which Vietnam was divided. A military 'Emergency' in Malaysia was declared as Chinese communists fought local people and British forces; a curfew was imposed on all ethnic Chinese during the Emergency.

Europe and the Near East saw the Suez Crisis, the Hungarian uprising and the Iron Curtain come firmly down between Eastern Europe and the West. In the former USSR discontent was brutally suppressed by sending 'offenders' and dissidents to labour camps, *gulags*. Solzhenitsyn (1974) chronicled this and describes the regime in his book *The Gulag Archipelago*.

The MacCarren Walter Act in 1952 severely limited the number of West Indians who could emigrate to seek work in the US, reducing it from 65 000 a year to 800. This meant that the British companies actively recruiting workers from the West Indies at this time were well received: 'There were adverts everywhere: Come to the Mother Country, the Mother Country needs you' (Harriott, 1991, p. 31).

Many immigrants who started looking for work in London found they had to move elsewhere in Britain in order to find employment. The majority did not expect to stay in Britain in their old age. They anticipated returning home after a period of earning good money in Britain.

They were also shocked at the 'welcome' they received:

> In Jamaica and in any other country where the white people are, we live together ... A person is just a person in spite of what colour they are. When we came here we thought it would be the same. But that is where the barriers come in. (W from Jamaica in Schweitzer, 1984, p. 29)

1950	Britain	Petrol costs 3 shillings (15p) per gallon. Bannister runs the 4-minute mile. A Labour Government is returned for a second term, without a working majority.
	India	Becomes a republic. India and Pakistan pledge to respect their minorities.
	China	Mao Tse Tung is established as the nation's leader. Land reforms take place.
	Tibet	Is occupied by China
	Korea	US General McArthur invades North Korea as part of his grander plan, to invade China.
1951	Britain	Meat rationing continues at 4oz per person per week.

The old-age pension is to be paid at 60 for women and 65 for men, not at 70 and 75 as previously.

The Festival of Britain aims to dispel the gloom of post-war austerity.

Churchill and the Tory Party come to power.

The first long-playing record (LP) is made.

West Indies
In Jamaica, 132 are killed in a hurricane. This persuades more people to emigrate to Britain.

Kenya
The Mau Mau, who are Kikuyu tribesmen who took a secret oath to kill and drive the white man out of Kenya, kill 95 European and 13 500 Africans before the British defeat them in 1956.

1952 Britain
King George VI dies.

Austerity continues although tea rationing ends.

Zebra crossings and Belisha beacons are officially launched.

Germany
Occupation by the Allies ends.

1953 Britain
Sweet rationing ends.

Queen Elizabeth II is crowned.

Car prices in Britain fall generally.

The Ford Popular becomes the world's cheapest 4-cylinder car at £390.

Former USSR
Stalin dies.

Korea
Thousands of British men are held amongst others as prisoners of war. As some are released, there is grave concern for their physical and mental health.

Nepal
Sir Edmund Hillary and Sherpa Tensing conquer Everest.

1954 Britain
Over three million attend Billy Graham's gospel meetings throughout Britain.

Rationing ends and people burn their ration books.

Myxomatosis wipes out the rabbit population.

French Indo-China
The war ends with a Chinese-French pact to divide Vietnam at the 17th parallel.

Cyprus
Nationalists revolt.

1955 Britain
Princess Margaret, the Queen's younger sister, agrees not to marry Captain Townsend, because he has been divorced.

Ports are closed by a dock strike.

China
A government campaign to uncover hidden counter-revolutionaries is launched.

1956	Britain	The Suez Crisis means petrol rationing is re-introduced.
	West Indies	London Transport starts recruiting staff in Barbados.
	Egypt	Nationalises the Suez Canal.
	Hungary	The Hungarian uprising is put down by Soviet troops.
1957	Ireland	A state of emergency is declared in Ireland because of the IRA.
1958	Britain	A plane crash in Munich kills seven of the Manchester United Team, known as the 'Busby Babes' and eight journalists.
		CND is formed.
		Yellow no-parking lines appear on Britain's roads for the first time.
	West Indies	The West Indian Federation is founded; its aim to bring economic and political benefits to the West Indies. (The initiative ended in 1962 after major disagreement between the participating countries.)
	China	The Great Leap Forward aims at creating economic and agricultural growth.
	The US	Americans put their first satellite into space.
	Ceylon	There are calls for better treatment for Tamils in Ceylon (Sri Lanka), and for a separate state.
1959	Britain	A revolutionary new car, the Mini, is launched. The M1, the first motorway, opens.
	West Indies	Communist revolution in Cuba. Cuba's close ties with USSR makes the US very nervous.
	China	Famine lasts until 1961.
	Tibet	There is a revolt against the occupying Chinese. The Dalai Lama, Tibet's religious leader flees the country.

1960–1969

This decade saw the first man in space and the first man on the moon. Spin-offs from space technology were domestic advances such as the non-stick frying pan and technological advances such as computer technology.

The US and Australia joined South Vietnam forces to fight against the Communist North.

In Hong Kong, thousands of Chinese emigrated to Britain, many starting Chinese restaurants and take-aways on their arrival.

The 'wind of change' swept through Africa and many African and West Indian countries gained independence, having been European colonies.

Black people in the US and in South Africa continued their struggle against racism and apartheid. The struggle was often violent and leaders were jailed (Mandela in South Africa) or murdered (Luther King in the US).

The civil rights movement in Northern Ireland sought equal rights for Catholics in the province.

The world came to the brink of a nuclear war during the Cuban missile crisis.

Youth culture continued to dominate in the West. The miniskirt became fashionable and very mini; dry cleaners charged for cleaning them by the inch, though by the end of the decade hemlines dropped.

The Beatles had a string of hits – 'She Loves You', 'Please Please Me', 'From Me to You', 'Beatlemania' sweeps Britain and the world. The 'Twist', a new dance, was popularised by Chubby Checker who claimed to have lost 39lbs dancing it.

James Bond became a cult figure as did *The Avengers* on television. *Monty Python's Flying Circus* is first shown by the BBC television.

1960	Britain	The unexpurgated version of D.H. Lawrence's book *Lady Chatterley's Lover* is published and is ruled by the Court as not obscene, overturning a previous ban on its publication.
	South Africa	All black political organisations are outlawed.
	Vietnam	US forces join the war in South Vietnam.
1961	Britain	The contraceptive pill is available on the NHS.
	India	Troops invade the Portuguese enclave of Goa, which has been Portuguese for 400 years.
	Germany	East Germany closes the Berlin Wall with barbed wire.
	Former USSR	Yuri Gagarin is the first man in space.
	South Africa	Nelson Mandela eludes a police round-up.

1962	Britain	MPs pass a Bill to restrict Commonwealth immigration.
		Fascist supporters march in London, and there is fighting in the East End.
	Ireland	In Northern Ireland the IRA calls off a five year campaign of violence. Britain frees jailed terrorists in response.
	India	Pandit Nehru is elected prime minister by a big majority.
		A state of emergency is declared when there is heavy fighting on the Chinese border.
		Students are urged to join the national cadet corps and people are asked to support India's war effort by giving their silver and gold ornaments for sale in exchange for foreign exchange.
	West Indies	Jamaica, Trinidad and Tobago become independent.
	The US	The Telstar satellite transmits transatlantic TV pictures.
		Marilyn Monroe dies, probably by suicide.
	Hong Kong	A barbed-wire fence is erected across the border with China to stop illegal immigrants coming in.
		Charter flights start to leave the colony packed with people hoping to make a new life in Britain.
	Cuba	The Cuban missile crisis puts the world on the brink of a nuclear war. President Kennedy of the US and the Russian leader Khrushchev face it out. The USSR finally backs down and Russian missiles are to be dismantled and removed from Cuba.
	South Africa	Nelson Mandela is jailed for five years.
	Nigeria	Becomes independent of Britain.
1963	Britain	The first successful kidney transplant is made, in Leeds.
		In the great train robbery at Cheddington, Buckinghamshire, the driver and guard are badly beaten up. The robbers get away with a haul worth a million pounds. Ronnie Biggs, one of the robbers, reappears later in South America.
	East Pakistan (Bangladesh)	Ten thousand people are killed in a cyclone; half a million are left homeless.
	The US	Black leader and clergyman Martin Luther King is arrested for a civil rights demonstration in Alabama.

		President John Kennedy is assassinated in Dallas by Lee Harvey Oswald who later is shot at point-blank range and killed by Jack Ruby. Both killings are seen live on television.
	Kenya	Gains independence from Britain and joins the Commonwealth.
1964	Britain	£10 bank notes are issued for the first time.
		BBC2 comes on the air: its first programme is *Playschool*.
		The first family planning clinic accepts unmarried couples.
		Teenage gangs of 'Mods' and 'Rockers' fight in seaside resorts during the year.
	Malta	Becomes independent of Britain.
	India	Two million people greet the Pope in Bombay.
		Seven thousand are killed in the Madras province by a hurricane.
		In Calcutta, 200 are killed in Hindu–Muslim riots.
	South Africa	Nelson Mandela is jailed for life.
	Cyprus	The UN peace-keeping force moves in as Greek and Turkish Cypriots fight; Turkish planes raid the north.
1965	Britain	Winston Churchill dies and is given a state funeral.
		The Beatles are given MBEs by the Queen; some people send their medals back in protest at the award being given to a pop group.
		Myra Hindley and Ian Brady are charged with the 'Moors Murders' of five or maybe more children. They are found guilty and get life imprisonment.
	East Pakistan (Bangladesh)	Ten thousand are killed in a violent cyclone.
	India	India and Pakistan clash over Kashmir.
	The US	American planes bomb Vietnam.
1966	Britain	A new fashion model, Twiggy, an Eastender who weighs 6½ stone, is the fashion image of the year.
		At Aberfan, 116 children and 28 adults are killed as a slag heap falls on the village and envelops their school.
	West Indies	London Transport recruit staff in Trinidad and in Jamaica.
		Barbados and Guyana become independent.

		Antigua and Barbuda, St Kitts-Nevis-Anguilla, Dominica, Grenada, St Lucia and St Vincent become an independent state associated with Britain.
	The US	Buzz Aldrin, astronaut, walks in space.
	China	Mao launches the Cultural Revolution. As students and soldiers wave their little red books, intellectuals, teachers and other intellectuals are given dunces' caps, rounded up and paraded through the streets in disgrace.
	Vietnam	Australia sends troops to Vietnam.
1967	Britain	Sir Francis Chichester, aged 65, sails round the world solo in Gypsy Moth IV. Liverpool's Catholic Cathedral, affectionately known as 'Paddy's Wigwam', is opened. Abortion is legalised.
	Hong Kong	Communist-inspired rioting causes the stock market and property prices to crash.
	South Africa	The first heart transplant is performed.
	Nigeria and Biafra	A civil war starts, continuing until 1969.
	Middle East	The Six Day War.
1968	Britain	First and second-class post is introduced by the Royal Mail. Enoch Powell makes an anti-immigration speech in Birmingham: 'As I look ahead I am filled with foreboding. Like the Roman I see the River Tiber foaming with much blood.' He is isolated by the Tory party but racists take to the street to reinforce his message.
	Ireland	One hundred Roman Catholics are hurt in Londonderry rioting.
	The US	Martin Luther King is shot dead. Violence and rioting ensues in the major cities.
	Kenya	The government takes Asians' trading licences away. Around 35 000 Asians who have Commonwealth-issue British passports are eventually allowed into Britain.
1969	Britain	The Queen invests Prince Charles as the Prince of Wales at Caernarvon Castle.
	Ireland	The 'Troubles' start with the first civil rights marches taking place in Londonderry. Roman Catholics cheer as British troops arrive. Belfast is set ablaze in rioting.

		Troops erect a peace wall between the Catholic Falls Road and the Protestant Shankill Road.
	The US	Neil Armstrong is the first man on the moon. Opposition to the Vietnam war increases.

1970–1979

Britain joined the EEC (Common Market). Equality between the sexes became an issue, all-male Oxford colleges admitting women students for the first time. Margaret Thatcher became Britain's first woman prime minister. The country celebrated the Queen's Silver Jubilee, many held street parties.

The Troubles escalated in Northern Ireland.

Idi Amin seized power in Uganda, committing many atrocities. He was finally deposed by Tanzanian troops.

There was rioting in South Africa.

Mozambique and Angola became independent of Portugal.

Bangladesh became independent of Pakistan. In 1979 an army coup took power in Pakistan.

The Vietnam War ended in 1975 and in 1978 Vietnam invaded Cambodia.

The Watergate scandal rocked the US. Initially President Nixon denied the allegations against him but finally admitted them and resigned.

1970	The US	The Black Power Movement is established.
1971	Britain	Decimal coinage introduced.
		'Hot pants' (very short tight shorts) are in fashion.
	Bangladesh	East Pakistan becomes independent of Pakistan. Two million people flee to India. India fights on the side of Bangladesh. Seven thousand people die; in the capital Dacca, dogs feed on the corpses.
	The US	Astronauts drive a buggy on the moon.
	Uganda	Idi Amin seizes power.
1972	Britain	Five Oxford colleges admit women for the first time.

	Ireland	Six are killed and 140 injured in a bomb attack in Belfast city centre.
	The US	American bombing brings North Vietnam to the conference table.
	Germany	The Olympic Games are held in Munich. Palestinians bomb the Israelis' buildings at the Munich Olympics. Two die.
	Uganda	President Idi Amin expels 50 000 Asians.
1973	Britain	Industry works a three-day week because a miners' strike has meant no coal supplies.
	West Indies	The Bahamas gain independence.
	Middle East	The Arab-Israeli war creates an economic crisis in Europe as oil supplies are cut and prices soar.
1974	Britain	The IRA bomb a coach full of soldiers and their families on the M62. Eleven die.
	Cyprus	Turkey invades Cyprus. A security zone is established. Greeks and Turks both flee to their 'safe' parts of the island leaving homes and possessions behind.
1975	Britain	Margaret Thatcher becomes the leader of the Tory Party. Charlie Chaplin is knighted. Dutch elm disease kills hundreds of thousands of elm trees, changing the face of the British countryside.
	West Indies	Gary Sobers, cricketer, is knighted by the Queen in Bridgetown. Angola and Mozambique are given independence by Portugal.
	Vietnam	Saigon, the capital of South Vietnam, falls to the Communists, and the war is over.
	Cambodia	The Khmer Rouge seize power, committing many atrocities and killing over two million people.
1976	Britain	A very hot summer. The Race Relations Act becomes law.
	China	Mao Tse Tung dies. The Gang of Four, who include Mao's widow, are condemned by the politburo as 'dog dung'.
	South Africa	Riots in Soweto.
	Canada	The Olympic Games are held in Montreal.
1977	Britain	The Queen and people throughout Britain celebrate her Silver Jubilee.
	Pakistan	Martial law is declared following an army coup, led by General Zia ul-Haq.

	Vietnam	The first 'boat people' leave Vietnam in large numbers.
	The US	Elvis Presley dies of a drug overdose.
1978	Britain	The first test-tube baby is born.
	Guyana	Followers of the Reverend Jim Jones commit mass suicide; 913 people die.
	Vietnam	Invades Cambodia.
1979	Britain	Margaret Thatcher becomes Britain's first woman Prime Minister.
	Ireland	Lord Mountbatten is killed by the IRA.
	West Indies	Anguilla separates from St Kitts-Nevis after unrest.
		The New Jewel Movement in Grenada, led by Maurice Bishop, brings the People's Revolutionary Government to power. The Government's sympathetic relations with Cuba make other Caribbean states and the US nervous. At the request of other Caribbean states US troops invade Grenada and remain there as a peacekeeping force until democratic elections in 1984.
	Pakistan	The ex-premier Bhutto is hanged by the current military government.
	Uganda	Tanzanian troops invade, Idi Amin is deposed.

1980–1989

At the begining of the decade, Britain celebrated the Royal Wedding, the wedding of the Prince and Princess of Wales. Margaret Thatcher was re-elected to power. Unemployment rose and at the same time the 'Yuppie' culture also grew. Britain fought the Falklands War against Argentina.

The Muslim world was very upset by the publication of Salman Rushdie's book *The Satanic Verses*. The book was burned in Britain and elsewhere and Rushdie went into hiding after death threats were issued against him.

President Gorbachev opened up the USSR.

China's relations with the outside world continued to relax, but they suffered a setback with the brutal crushing of the student demonstrations in Tiananmen Square, which were seen by millions on television.

Tourism grew in the West Indies, becoming one of its major industries.

The AIDS epidemic began its sweep through the world, initially in the US and Africa, then Europe and the former USSR and then the Far East.

1980	The US	John Lennon is shot dead in New York.
	Former USSR	The Olympic Games are held in Moscow.
	Zimbabwe	Formerly known as Rhodesia becomes independent.
	Iran/Iraq	War begins.
1981	Britain	Prince Charles marries Lady Diana Spencer.
		Peter Sutcliffe, the 'Yorkshire Ripper', is convicted of killing thirteen women in four years.
1982	Britain	Three million are unemployed.
		The Falklands War.
		Channel Four goes on air.
	Sri Lanka	Government forces fight the Tamil separatists.
	Israel	Invades Lebanon.
1983	Britain	Margaret Thatcher is re-elected as Prime Minister.
	West Indies	Anguilla becomes independent.
1984	Britain	York Minster is gutted by fire.
		Boy George becomes a pop idol.
		The IRA bomb the hotel where party leaders are staying for the Tory Party conference in Brighton.
		A patient dies of AIDS after a blood transfusion.
	India	Prime Minister Mrs Gandhi is assassinated by Sikh terrorists.
	The US	The Olympic Games are held in Los Angeles.
1985	Britain	Bob Geldof organises the Live Aid concert.
	Former USSR	Gorbachev becomes leader.
1986	The US	The *Challenger* spacecraft explodes on take-off.
	Former USSR	The Chernobyl nuclear plant explodes, it will be some time before the full impact of the damage is known.
1987	Britain	The cross-channel ferry SS *Herald of Free Enterprise* sinks; two hundred are killed.
		Salman Rushdie publishes *The Satanic Verses*. The Muslim world is very upset by the publication and death threats are issued against Rushdie.

		A gunman goes berserk in the market town of Hungerford, Berkshire: fourteen die, fifteen are wounded.
		The storm of the century strikes in October: thousands of trees are knocked over, many houses are badly damaged.
		The bottom falls out of the stock market.
1988	West Indies	Hurricane Gilbert causes major damage, especially in Jamaica.
1989	Britain	Bradford Muslims burn Rushdie's book *The Satanic Verses*. He goes into hiding.
		Ninety-four people die in the Hillsborough football stadium disaster.
		Trouble flares at the Notting Hill Carnival.
	West Indies	Michael Manley is elected as Jamaica's prime minister.
	China	Troops massacre protesters in Tiananmen Square.
	The US	Is hit by the biggest-ever oil spill, when the SS *Exxon Valdez* runs aground, spilling eleven million tons of crude oil into Prince William Sound, Alaska.
	Former USSR	'Gorbymania' hits new heights as Gorbachev tours West Germany.
	Germany	The Berlin Wall comes down.
	Romania	Ceausescu and his wife are executed by firing squad. The truth about the lives of ordinary people and the orphanages in which they had no option but to put their children is gradually revealed.

REFERENCES

Bygott, D. 1992. *Black and British*. Oxford University Press.

Chang, Jung. 1993. *Wild Swans*, Flamingo.

Durrell, Lawrence. 1957. *Bitter Lemons of Cyprus*, Faber and Faber.

Fyson, Nance Lui. 1989. *World in View: Hong Kong*, Macmillan.

Griffiths, John. 1989. *The Caribbean*, Wayland.

Harriott, J. 1991. *Black Women in Britain*, Batsford.

Lamb, D. 1984. *The Africans*, Vintage.

Mercer, D. ed. 1988. *Chronicle of the Twentieth Century*, Chronicle.

Middleton, H., Heater, D. 1989. *Atlas of Modern World History*, Oxford University Press.

Morris, Jan. 1988. *Hong Kong: Epilogue to an Empire*, Penguin.

Nugent, N. 1992. *World in View: Pakistan and Bangladesh*, Macmillan.

Robertson, Ian 1990. *Blue Guide – Cyprus*, A & C Black.

Rushdie, Salman. 1982. *Midnight's Children*, Picador.
Schweitzer, Pam. ed. 1984. *A Place to Stay: Memories of Pensioners from Many Lands*, Age Exchange Theatre Company.
Solzhenitsyn, A. 1974. *The Gulag Archipelago*, Fontana.
Thubron, Colin. 1986. *Journey into Cyprus*, Penguin.

Events index

Numbers in brackets refer to the year (or the decade) under which the event appears on the page indicated.

Subject index

Africa
  books on 89
  videos 90
Afro-Caribbean groups, examples
    of reminiscence 20–21
Age Concern 82, 83
Age Exchange 82
Ageing
  differing rates of 1
  disabilities associated with 5
  factors in 1
  positive approach to 2
  see also Mental health problems
Ages of man, a fourth age 2
Anger, right to express 27
Assessment of the elderly
  assessment schemes 9
  by local authorities 4–5
Audio recordings, for life history
    books 58

Bangladesh, geography, history
    and culture 94–7
BASE (British Association for
    Services to the Elderly) 82
Belfast, HMS 83
Bereavement 6–7
Black groups, examples of
    reminiscence 20–21
Books
  on Black Africa 89
  on the Caribbean 89
  on China and Hong Kong 89
  on grief and death 86–7
  on history and mythology 90
  on India and Pakistan 89–90
  large print 90
  on life in Britain and France 88

on lives of old people 87–8
on mental and physical health
    85–6
on people in society 85
on war 88–9
on ways of working with old
    people 87
on working with old people
    85–7
Britain, life in
  books on 88
  videos 91
Britain at War Theme Museum 83
British Association for Services to
    the Elderly (BASE) 82

Carers
  distress to 54
  fears of effect of reminiscence
    23–4
  need for 54
  need for sensitive listening 56
  support for 54
Caribbean
  books on 89
  geography, history and culture
    99–101
China, books on 89
Churches, and reminiscence work
    84
Clifton Assessment Procedures for
    the Elderly (CAPE) 9
Communication
  covert and latent 47
  cross-cultural 27–9
  across generations 27, 29
  helping with expression of
    feelings 26–7

Ageing, Healthy and in Control

An alternative approach to maintaining the health of older people

S Scrutton, Social Work Manager,
Northamptonshire Social Services Department, UK

This book challenges conventional approaches to meeting the health needs of older people. It examines the neglect, despair and pessimism that so often surround the subject. 'Medicalization' of caring for older people, which so often appears to remove them from personal responsibility for their own health, is also discussed.

The book recommends that older people, sometimes with the support of carers, take a more pro-active role in the maintenance of health as they grow older. It does this by: critically examining the role of conventional medical ideas and practice, particularly in relation to the health of older people; promoting the idea of self-help through exercise, nutrition, continuing social engagement and the adoption of practical, preventative measures in an individual's lifestyle; examining the potential value and benefit to older people of many alternative medical disciplines such as homoeopathy, herbal medicine, acupuncture and others.

Key Features

* directed at the over 65 age group

* analyses conventional health treatment and reviews complementary therapies

* focuses on the subject of ageism and how this affects the health of older people

Contents: Nature and the importance of good health in old age. Medical ageism: expectations of health in old age. Allopathic medicine: the medicalization of old age. An holistic approach: the causes of illness in old age. Escaping the psychology of medical ageism: reasserting personal control. Maintaining social engagement: combating loneliness and loss. Diet and nutrition. Physical aspects of good health: exercise, posture and relaxation. Alternative medicine: the fall and rise of traditional medical practice. Treating the illnesses of old age. An approach to loss, death and dying. The role of the professional carer. Useful addresses. References. Index.

Therapy in Practice Series 29
(Series Editor: Jo Campling)

August 1992: 216x138: 240pp Paperback: 0-412-38890-1: £12.95

CHAPMAN & HALL

Elder Abuse

Concepts, theories and interventions

G Bennett, Consultant Geriatrician, Royal London Hospital, UK and
P Kingston, Lecturer in Nursing, North Staffordshire College of Nursing, UK

The concept of elder abuse and neglect as a social problem continues to remain elusive. A major impediment has been the absence of research and clear definition of the problem, and a book which summarises what is known about elder abuse has been needed for a long time. Drawing on examples from the US and the UK, this book is a major contribution to research and information currently available.

The authors define elder abuse broadly. While physical abuse is one aspect of the problem, Bennet and Kingston also study financial, emotional, sexual and psychological abuse and neglect. In addition, they cover practical concerns and recognition, intervention, prevention, and related legal issues. With its multidisciplinary approach, the book is appropriate for nurses, occupational therapists, physiotherapists, social workers, geriatricians, and all other health care professionals involved in elderly care.

* elder abuse and inadequate care is one of the main social/medical issues of the 1990s

* a multidisciplinary approach, including nursing, social work, therapy, medicine

* incorporates examples from UK and USA

Contents: Foreword. Introduction. Historical background: definitions and theories. The abused and the abuser. Recognition and assessment of abuse/inadequate care. Intervention. Legal issues. Health and social service cooperation. Prevention. Institution abuse and neglect. Research. Index.

Therapy in Practice Series 39
(Series Editor: Jo Campling)

October 1993: 216x138: c.184pp, 4 line illus, 4 halftone illus Paperback: 0-412-45310-X: £14.95

CHAPMAN & HALL

Practical Psychiatry of Old Age

Second Edition

J Wattis, and **C Martin**,
Academic Unit of Psychiatry, University of Leeds, UK

Reviews from the First Edition:

"...this book will become very popular. Like the best vade mecums it combines theory and practice in an easily accessible and comprehensible fashion. Workers from many disciplines will find it useful and will want to buy it."
British Medical Journal

The main focus of this new edition remains the practical assessment and management of people presenting with psychiatric symptoms in late life. The core of the book describes the common presentations of depression, confusion, somatic preoccupation, hallucinations and delusions. Case vignettes are used to illustrate the approach to clinical problems. There is special emphasis on the complex interaction of social, psychological and medical factors and the need for close multi-disciplinary teamwork. The new edition has been revised to: update the clinical approach, update patient management under new policies, provide a precise diagnostic system and structure the book in keeping with today's practice.

* illustrated with many clinical examples

* considers psychological, social and medical interventions

* emphasizes thorough assessment as the key to good management

* describes a practical approach to multi-disciplinary management

* text is built around the common clinical presentations of psychiatric disorders of old age

Contents: Introduction. Assessment. The classification of mental illness in old age. Mood disorder: depression and mania. Confusion. Somatization and hypochondriasis. Hallucinations and persecutory states. Psychological therapy with older people. Pharmacological treatment and ECT. The organization of legal services and the law in relation to treatment. Index.

October 1993: 216x138: c.264pp, 26 line illus, Paperback: 0-412-47460-3: £14.95

CHAPMAN & HALL

Old Age in Modern Society

2nd Edition

A textbook of social gerontology

C Victor, Department of Public Health Medicine, Parkside Health Authority, UK

From a review of the previous edition:
"This book merits a place in every Department of Public Health,
and every Social Services Department" - Public Health

Old age is part of the life cycle about which there are numerous myths and stereotypes. The appropriateness or otherwise of these myths is evaluated by Christina Victor using detailed statistical material from a biographical and anthropological perspective.

The new edition of this readable and thoughtful review of the present and future needs of the elderly provides an up-to-date overview of the position of older people in late 20th century Britain. It examines their social and economic circumstances and the main policy issues including pensions, housing, health and social care.

Data from Britain and other countries complete the revision of this standard work for social and health workers, sociologists and social policy analysts at both undergraduate and postgraduate levels. A wide audience will find this a useful introduction to the characteristics of older people in a modern industrial society.

Contents: Introduction to the study of ageing. Approaches to the study of ageing. Methodological aspects of the study of ageing. Historical and cultural perspectives on ageing. Images of ageing. The demography of ageing. Housing and the elderly. Work and retirement. Standards of living. Family and social networks. Health and illness. Services for the elderly. Issues in the politics of ageing. Bibliography.

» contains the latest statistical census material to provide the reader with all the statistics they need on social gerontology

» provides an up-to-date overview of the position of older people in late 20th century Britain

» examines the main policy issues: pensions, housing, health and social care to give a clear guide to policy decisions

April 1994: 234x156: c.288pp
Paperback: 0-412-54350-8: £19.99

CHAPMAN & HALL